GROWING POINTS IN THEOLOGY

OLD TESTAMENT COVENANT

OLD TESTAMENT COVENANT

A Survey of Current Opinions

DENNIS J. McCARTHY, S.J.

OXFORD
BASIL BLACKWELL
1973

q

Printed in Great Britain by
Compton Printing Ltd., Aylesbury
and bound by the Kemp Hall Bindery, Oxford

335710

Preface

This study has had something of an Odyssey. A much shorter form of it appeared in *The Catholic Biblical Quarterly* 27 (1965), 217–40. The body of this book is a version of a German form, *Der Gottesbund im Alten Testament*. Stuttgarter Bibelstudien 13². Stuttgart, 1967.

The present version will make the material available to the English reader. Wherever possible, therefore, reference has been made to English versions of the literature, but it is still necessary to take into account a large amount of work which is available only in foreign languages. It will perhaps be of some service to those who do not use these languages to have access to at least a short review of this work in their own tongue.

In addition, while there has been no attempt at an exhaustive survey of material relevant to covenant which has appeared since the German edition, a Postscript does treat as much that is significant as has come to my attention since then. In the Postscript the order of the original chapters is followed. By referring to it the reader can easily discover the present state of the question on the various topics involved.

DENNIS J. McCARTHY, S.J.

St. Louis University Divinity School,
St. Louis, Missouri, U.S.A.
11 June 1969.

Abbreviations

ANET	*Ancient Near Eastern Texts relating to the Old Testament*
ATANT	*Abhandlungen zur Theologie des Alten und Neuen Testaments*
BA	*The Biblical Archaeologist*
BASOR	*Bulletin of the American Schools of Oriental Research*
BBB	*Bonner Biblische Beiträge*
BWANT	*Beiträge zur Wissenschaft des Alten und Neuen Testaments*
BZ	*Biblische Zeitschrift*
BZAW	*Beihefte zur Zeitschrift für die Alttestamentliche Wissenschaft*
CBQ	*The Catholic Biblical Quarterly*
FRLANT	*Forschungen zur Religion und Literatur des Alten und Neuen Testaments*
JAOS	*Journal of the American Oriental Society*
JBL	*Journal of Biblical Literature*
JCS	*Journal of Cuneiform Studies*
JNES	*Journal of Near Eastern Studies*
JSS	*Journal of Semitic Studies*
JTS	*Journal of Theological Studies*
MDOG	*Mitteilungen der Deutschen Orient-Gesellschaft*
RB	*Revue biblique*
SANT	*Studien zum Alten und Neuen Testament*
TLZ	*Theologische Literaturzeitung*
VT	*Vetus Testamentum*
VTSuppl	*Supplements to Vetus Testamentum*
WMANT	*Wissenschaftliche Monographien zum Alten und Neuen Testament*
ZAW	*Zeitschrift für die Alttestamentliche Wissenschaft*
ZTK	*Zeitschrift für Theologie und Kirche*

Contents

I

The Concept of Covenant

We do not know for sure why the Septuagint chose the rather unusual *diathēkē*, 'testament', to translate the Hebrew *berît*, 'covenant'; somehow, this makes the translation and its fate symbolic. Covenant is so important in the Scriptures that in the form 'testament' it has provided the title for the book, but it is so complex an idea that we have our problems in understanding it.

As so often we may orientate ourselves best by reference to the great nineteenth-century critic, Julius Wellhausen. One of the arguments he uses to establish his view of a strictly evolutionary development of O.T. religion is precisely the development of the idea of covenant as he sees it. For Wellhausen covenant is indeed an ancient concept, but at the beginning it is one of a low order. He conceives of the original state of the covenanted people in terms that may best be described as totemism. The covenant between Israel and Yahweh meant that Israel was literally the son of God and somehow physically shared in the divine nature. This was supposed to be the status of a typical primitive religion with parallels in the religions studied by anthropologists the world over, so that Israel began no differently from other peoples with an idea of a blood relationship to its God. According to Wellhausen, it is only the prophetic movement with its 'ethical monotheism' which developed a sense of covenant suitable to a higher religion, namely, the idea that union with God is not a matter of natural relationship or magical rite but of morality. Israel is the special friend, the covenant partner of God, because and only so long as it keeps his law. Wellhausen sees here a great and important development in the history of religion. The original, crude, materialistic concept of the family of Yahweh has become a higher religion in which morality is all.

The views of Wellhausen were widely influential but by no means acceptable to all scholars. Many theologians were embarrassed by what they took to be the legalism of the later development of the covenant idea as described by Wellhausen. It seemed to make a religion of law and to smack of the Pharisaism which was condemned by the Gospels and by Saint Paul. Covenant was a kind of contract between God and the people through which the people earned God's friendship and protection by their keeping of the law. Could the revealed religion of the O.T. be an affair of law and not gospel, the pure grace given to depraved man?[1]

Philology and berît

Such was the status of the idea of covenant and some of its theological implications a generation or two ago. The effort to develop or to redefine the concept of covenant was largely confined to philological investigation, to the study of the use and meaning of the word, *berît*, 'covenant', in the Old Testament. A typical and very influential effort was that of Begrich, published in 1944, in which he concluded that the basic and original meaning of *berît* was that of a legal union (*Rechtsgemeinschaft*) which was established by a simple act of the will on the part of the more powerful party. In the concrete this would be represented by the sort of thing we find in the O.T. concerning Abraham or David. God simply promises his special protection and a special union between the human party and himself without any conditions or demands made upon the subordinate party and without any expression of a willing acceptance on the side of that party.[2] W. Schottroff argues to a similar onesidedness in some aspects of covenant thinking since the important phrase *zkr berît* implies an appeal to the divine overlord simply as the generous giver of a covenant without any reference to Israel's having kept the covenant.[3]

[1] For example, see the discussion in H. Wheeler Robinson, *Inspiration and Revelation in the Old Testament*, Oxford, 1946, 153–5.

[2] 'berit. Ein Beitrag zur Erfassung einer alttestamentlichen Denkform', *ZAW* 60 (1944), 1–11 (=*Gesammelte Studien zum Alten Testament*, ed. by W. Zimmerli, München, 1964, pp. 55–66).

[3] W. Schottroff, *'Gedenken' im Alten Orient und im Alten Testament*, *WMANT* 15, Neukirchen, 1964, 202–24.

Taken in an absolute sense, as though the unconditioned covenant were the normal, 'pure' form of covenant (and Begrich is often so taken), this is unrealistic. All covenants, all contracts, have their conditions. They must be defined somehow or other. These definitions are their conditions or stipulations which may often be assumed, things which are simply so well known in a culture that they need not be stated explicitly. For instance many societies have the idea of a brotherhood which is formed literally by the mingling of one another's blood through cuts and so on. The conditions of such a brotherhood are often rigidly defined by custom, but the partners need not make this definition explicit when they become 'brothers'.[4] But the idea that God alone grants the covenant and that covenant is essentially his grace may well be retained. The people do not earn it. The almighty Yahweh imposes it. It has been pointed out that so true is this in certain cases that the human partner to the covenant could even be asleep as God made the covenant (Gen. 15:9–12, 17–18), but even here the man, Abraham, must eventually respond to the divine gift.[5]

Further philological investigations came from L. Köhler. He thought that the characteristic phrase *krt bᵉrît* ('cut a covenant') indicates a covenant between equals, while the form *krt bᵉrît lᵉ-/ᵉim* ('cut a covenant for/with') indicates a covenant granted by a superior. Another common phrase, *hqym bᵉrît* ('raise up a covenant'), is used for making a covenant with God because He is sure to keep it (i.e., make it stand up). The essential word itself, *bᵉrît*, is related to the root *brh* which indicates food and eating. Hence he holds that the original idea of covenant stemmed from the covenant meal, and that the characteristic phrase 'cut a covenant' grew up because one had to cut up food for the covenant meal.[6]

---

[4] For instance, the covenants of Abimelech with Abraham (Gen.21;22–32) and with Isaac (Gen. 26, 26–31) do not specify what 'deal falsely' or 'do harm' mean, surely because this was understood: cf. D. J. McCarthy, S.J., 'Three Covenants in Genesis', *CBQ* 26 (1964), 179–89. See also E. Gerstenberger, *Wesen und Herkunft des 'Apodiktischen Rechts'*, *WMANT* 20, Neukirchen, 145–6, on the inseparability of covenant and commandment.

[5] G. Jacob, 'Der Abraham-Bund (Eine Bibelarbeit zu 1. Mose 15)', *Communio viatorum* 7 (1964), 250–4.

[6] L. Köhler, 'Problems in the Study of the Language of the Old Testament', *JSS* 1 (1956), 4–7.

Recently A. Jepsen has studied the word *berît* again and has concluded that it does not refer to a legal unity or community (so Begrich). Rather it refers to the very act that produces the relationship and not directly to the relationship itself. Further, his investigation does not bear out Begrich's conclusion that the original and truest form of covenant must be a simple grant by the superior without any conditions. Rather he finds that even in very early forms of covenant, conditions were often present and that covenant was often enough instituted by the inferior. However, he emphasizes that in the primary form of the important covenant, that between God and Israel, it was indeed the superior alone who granted the covenant.[7]

Progress beyond lexicography recently has come from investigation of covenant in the light of formal and comparative literary studies. Nevertheless, the word studies are important because they do admit a development of the idea of covenant in the O.T., and they are conscious that the idea of covenant is not univocal. A certain amount of current investigation of covenant sometimes seems to treat covenant as a univocal concept throughout the O.T.; wherever a covenant is mentioned, it is assumed to have had certain characteristics which pertain to *one* form of covenant. However, it is simply a fact that there are many different forms of covenant and these different forms imply different meanings.

Covenant and Biblical Theology

A different treatment of covenant is that of Walter Eichrodt in his *Theology of the Old Testament*. He defines covenant in terms of its theological meaning and sees it as the central theme of the O.T. as a theological book. He finds that the covenant concept implies that God's relation with Israel and consequently the religion of Israel must be historical; he notes that the covenant also contains an expression of the will and desires of the principal partner and that this provided Israel with a knowledge of the divine will, a law, which guided its actions and gave it a feeling of confidence in a milieu in which the divine was usually felt to be arbitrary and terrifying. Finally he recognizes that the covenant as a gift of

[7] A. Jepsen, 'berith. Ein Beitrag zur Theologie der Exilzeit', *Rudolph Festschrift*, Tübingen, 1961, 161–80; R. Smend, *Die Bundesformel*, *Theologische Studien* 68, Zürich, 1963, 26–7, points out that this is true of the Deuteronomic school except for Deut. 26:17–18.

God could be withdrawn and perhaps would be if Israel failed in its duty to the covenant.[8]

Eichrodt's work has been very influential. This is in part because he '. . . provides a remarkably comprehensive and illuminating summary of the religious ideas contained in the Old Testament',[9] in part because a number of his ideas seem to have been confirmed by the discovery of the parallels between Israelite covenant and the ancient treaty which we shall see in the next section. Nonetheless, his work '. . . is certainly not . . . invulnerable to criticism, and this concerns not merely details of interpretation, but reaches down to the very foundations of the whole presentation. Since the Old Testament is not a collection of writings which set out to provide a systematic summary of religious doctrines. Eichrodt is forced to proceed by a method of inference. Thus, for example, the importance of the great Deuteronomistic historical work (Joshua—2 Kings) is found not in the history with which it deals, nor in the interpretation which it places upon this history, but in the incidental allusions to the religious ideas of its leading characters, and, indirectly, of its author. What can be inferred about the beliefs of ancient Israelites becomes more significant than the plain statements which the Old Testament contains. Eichrodt's theology is, at bottom, an attempt to reconstruct the basic ideas current in ancient Israelite religion, rather than an assessment of the theological meaning of the Old Testament in the literary form in which we now possess it. The method of approach to the subject as a whole greatly affects the detailed interpretation of the Old Testament material. Eichrodt accepts, for example, that there is basically one essential covenant doctrine in the Old Testament, pointing to Moses and Mount Sinai, and he makes little or no attempt to assess the very different covenant theologies that the Old Testament contains. The historical relationships, and ideological differences, of the Abrahamic, Mosaic and Davidic covenants are glossed over in the necessity to subordinate the entire Old Testament material to the one covenant of Mount Sinai. Similarly, it is doubtful whether early Israelites were

[8] *Theology of the Old Testament*, London, 1961.
[9] R. E. Clements, 'The Problem of OT theology', *The London Quarterly and Holborn Review*, Jan. 1965, 12–13. The immediately following quotation in the text is from the same source.

always as conscious of the Sinai covenant in their worship, as Eichrodt claims.' In other words, this theology of the O.T. forces the O.T. concept of covenant into a single form, when it had many, and does not do justice to the complex history of the idea in the O.T.

Covenant as Idea and as Institution

The more recent ideas about covenant which will be discussed in the following chapter have developed only when the rather one-sided investigation of the concept of covenant was supplemented by studies of covenant from the point of view of the cult, history, and sociology. Thus S. Mowinckel developed the idea that celebrating the renewal of the covenant was central to the Israelite cult. His studies of the psalms led to the conclusion that recalling the covenant was an important part of the feast we know as Tabernacles.[10] Mowinckel believed this to have been originally a New Year festival at which Yahweh was acclaimed king, as in the so-called 'kingship of Yahweh' psalms.[11] Note that he does not hold that there was an annual restoration of Yahweh, as do some of the more radical members of the patternist and royal-ideologist schools. Rather there was a renewed acknowledgment of Yahweh's continuing supremacy. Along with creation the concrete basis for this sovereignty was considered to be the covenant made with the Patriarchs and renewed at Sinai (Vol. 1, p. 157). In the manner of the cult this basis was made present again in the ceremonies and words (technically, 'myths', i.e., words accompanying a rite which may represent historical realities) of the festival (Vol. 2, pp. 249–50). Further, the introduction of the Decalogue, 'I am Yahweh, your God', is a sentence connected with the representation of a theophany, which was central to the New Year rite. Since the proclamation of the divine will commonly accompanied the theophany, it was natural that the expression of this will, eventually summarized in the Decalogue, be part of the rite and so be connected with covenant and its renewal (Vol. 1, p. 158; Vol. 2, p. 70).

[10] *The Psalms in Israel's Worship*, Nashville, 1962, Oxford, 1963, 2 vols. All references are to this, Mowinckel's latest expression relating to the problem, but much can be found more fully argued in his earlier works; *Psalmenstudien*, Oslo, 1921–24, 5 vols (reprinted, Amsterdam, 1966), and *Le Décalogue*, Paris, 1927.   [11] Pss. 47, (81), 93, (95), 96–9.

Not all of Mowinckel's ideas have been accepted, but his emphasis on the central importance of the cult for the study of Israel's traditions is surely correct, and it has proved fruitful. So, independently of the details of Mowinckel's reconstructed *Bundesfest*, it is widely accepted that the covenant law was the object of a public liturgical manifestation. In Deut. 31:9 ff., Moses directs that 'this law' (i.e., Deuteronomy) is to be read aloud at the feast of Tabernacles every seven years. Surely it is impossible that the whole book of Deuteronomy have been read aloud, but it seems likely that this Deuteronomic direction is an adaptation of a real custom of reading at regular intervals some shorter form of religious law such as the Decalogue.[12] Thus the relics of ancient Israelite practice indicate that a law connected with covenant was carried in a regular ceremony. It had its organs of transmission and interpretation (the cult personnel) and it is obviously aimed at commanding obedience, at guiding the believing community. It was thus institutionalized, i.e., organized, structured and public.

Scholars have gone further still. Faced with the apparent diversity of Israelite origins as indicated by the complex early history of the tribes. they have sought to piece together the outline of the process by which unity was achieved. Here the most influential idea has been that of M. Noth, who pointed out the resemblance of the tribal organization of Israel at the time of the judges to the institution known from Greek examples as an amphictyony.[13] This resemblance appears in the possession of a common cult centre (Shechem, Gilgal, Shiloh) around which twelve more or less autonomous tribes united for common acts,

[12] See A. Alt, 'The Origins of Israelite Law', *Essays on Old Testament History and Religion*, Oxford, 1966, 103–71: K. Baltzer, *Das Bundesformular*, 16–17. G. von Rad, 'The Form-Critical Problem of the Hexateuch', *The Problem of the Hexateuch and Other Essays*, Edinburgh, 1966, 1–78, is a very influential study of the connection between this liturgical reading of the law, the recitation of Yahweh's saving acts, and the development of Israel's traditions into the great Pentateuchal sources and eventually the Pentateuch itself. A. Weiser, *The Psalms*, London, 1959, has in its introduction and *passim* a discussion of a covenant feast not entirely unlike Mowinckel's, but without the emphasis on royal elements.
[13] *Das System der zwölf Stämme Israels*, *BWANT* IV, 1. Berlin, 1930: for a discussion in English, see M. Noth, *The History of Israel*,[2] New York, 1960, 53–109.

worship and war. This is like the twelve Greek city states formed into the Delphic league, and, perhaps, the league of an original six (?) Philistine cities. It is important to the argument that an amphictyony be necessarily constituted by a group of six or a multiple of that number, for then not merely the grouping of a heterogeneous mass under the name Israel but also the insistence on the rather artificial number of twelve tribes is explained by the amphictyony concept. A further point in favour of the hypothesis of an Israelite amphictyony is its explanation of the enigmatic 'minor judges' (Judg. 10:1–5; 12:7–15) as 'law-speakers' who preserved the common code of the alliance and proclaimed it to the tribes assembled periodically at the cult centre.

This brilliant hypothesis has received almost universal acceptance. It is the basis on which much further discussion of the Israelite covenant with Yahweh has proceeded. Still, serious doubts have been raised. R. Smend holds that the supposed amphictyonic union of the Hebrew tribes in the pre-monarchical era, a union based on covenant with a common God, was not the primary actual unifying force in Israel. Rather it was the Holy War which produced active unity.[14] He argues from the fact that the essential covenant formula: 'I, Yahweh, am your God, and you are my people', is not attested before the monarchy and probably not before Deuteronomy. The pre-monarchical Song of Deborah (Judg. 5) shows that the tribes became Yahweh's people only when they joined together in the Holy War; those who remained aloof from the fight were not Yahweh's people (Judg. 5:3, 5). The evidence from the song also gives only ten tribes as possible members of the union, a fact which is embarrassing if six or a multiple thereof was an indispensable feature of an amphictyonic grouping. In fact, it was only gradually and under the necessity to counter pressure from outside by joining together in war that the covenanted union of all Israel came to be formed.[15] Rather than being the centre around which Israel's history was played in the era before the kingdom, the covenanted union, the

[14] R. Smend, *Die Bundesformel, Theologische Studien* 68, Zurich, 1963, and *Jahwekrieg und Stämmebund, FRLANT* 84, Göttingen, 1963: in the latter he speaks of unity *in potency* (covenant) and *in act* (war), and he shows how doubtful it is to speak of the ark and/or Shechem as the central cult object or shrine. On the Holy War see G. von Rad, *Der Heilige Krieg im alten Israel*,[3] Göttingen, 1958.

[15] *Bundesformel*, 11–13, 19, 21.

amphictyony if you will, was the result of the historical working out of the Holy War.

There is a further problem with the fact that a palladium, the ark of the covenant, rather than a shrine, is supposed to have been the cultic centre of the Israelite amphictyony. This departs from the normal state of things in the Greek and Italian amphictyonies. So does the fact that the cultic centre was subject to frequent change—Shechem, Gilgal, and Shiloh do not exhaust the list of the proposed centres. Finally, the necessity for an organization of twelve (or six) tribes, held to be one of the chief positive arguments for an amphictyonic structure, is not really compelling. In fact, ancient custom does not seem to have insisted on such numbers.[16]

[16] The argument is developed in B. D. Rahtjen, 'Philistine and Hebrew Amphictyonies', *JNES* 24 (1965), 100–4. See also J. Bright, *A History of Israel*, Philadelphia, 1959, 147, and J. R. Porter, *Moses and Monarchy*, Oxford, 1963, 26–7, on the problems involved with accepting Shechem as the centre of an Israelite amphictyony, although the assumption of an amphictyony is bound up with accepting Shechem as just this.

2

Covenant as Treaty

Considerable impetus has been given the study of the covenant between Yahweh and Israel by the apparent analogy between parts of the Old Testament and ancient Near Eastern texts. By far the most important has been the comparison with treaty texts, especially those between sovereigns and vassals. These treaties reveal a form of covenant which has many of the characteristics which Eichrodt, starting from his purely theological point of view, found in the Old Testament covenant between God and the chosen people. The first important exploration of the analogy between the treaties and Israel's covenant was George Mendenhall's *Law and Covenant in Israel and the Ancient Near East*.[1] Since so much other work has depended on this pioneering effort, it is important to consider it at some length.

Covenant and Law in Israel

According to Mendenhall the very unity of the Israelite people and its relationship with God was founded on covenant, and this covenant was in its original form a purely religious affair; as in all agreements or covenants between persons there was implied or expressed a condition which is really a description of the sort of relationship into which they are entering and which appears as law. In Israel's original condition this set of laws with their sanctions was purely religious. There was no civil machinery to enforce the law (p. 23). With the coming of the monarchy the legal traditions of the covenanted folk, the amphictyony, were

[1] Pittsburgh, 1955 (*BA* 17 (1954), 26–46, 49–76). All references in the text are to the separate publication. See now also G. Mendenhall, 'Covenant', *Interpreter's Dictionary of the Bible*, Vol. 1, 714–23.

taken over or rather displaced by the activity of the king and his
courts. It was necessary for the monarchy to have a civil structure with its laws and agencies of enforcement, and often this
structure was in conflict with the law of the covenant (pp. 17–19,
44–7). However, during the period of the monarchy the prophets
kept alive the true idea of covenant and their preaching was
essentially a prosecution of Israel for its failure to live up to the
true covenant (pp. 19, 46–7). Finally, the Deuteronomic reform
returned to the ancient Mosaic concept of the covenanted people.
This was a true reformation in which Israel turned aside from
the aberrations of the monarchy and returned to the true word of
the covenant which had been given by Moses (pp. 47–9).

Thus Prof. Mendenhall explains the character of Israelite law,
which uses the traditions of ancient Semitic civil law—traditions
appearing in Israel in the form of the famous case laws—but also
has its own special form, the apodictic laws, the absolute commands. These latter are the direct results of the covenant tradition. Yahweh, the sovereign, has commanded his covenanted
people, his vassals, in absolute terms. This law then has, as the
O.T. constantly asserts, an essentially religious sanction. This
law is the result of, or better, the very definition of the covenant
relationship, a religious relationship between Israel and its God.

Covenant and History

Besides his explanation of the Israelite law and its characteristics,
Mendenhall's study has enabled him to construct an interpretation of the history of Israel in terms of an original covenant
mediated by Moses, then a falling away from this early, pure
Mosaic covenant under and because of the monarchy, in which
the religious community tried to become a civil community and
so was corrupted, and finally a reform, a return to something like
the pure Mosaic tradition of the covenant. This whole interpretation of Israelite law and history depends on Mendenhall's
first step—the dating of the Decalogue to the time of Moses—
which he accomplishes by the comparison with the Hittite vassal
treaties. Basing his work upon the study of V. Korošec, *Hethitische Staatsverträge*,[2] Mendenhall presents this outline of the
Hittite treaty:

[2] *Leipziger rechtswissenschaftliche Studien* 60, Leipzig, 1931. The
primary concern in most of the work dependent upon this study has been

1. Preamble introducing the sovereign;
2. The historical prologue describing previous relations between the contracting parties;
3. The stipulations which outline the nature of the community formed by the covenant;
4. The document clause providing for preservation and regular re-reading of the treaty;
5. The list of gods who witnessed the treaty;
6. The curse and blessing formula, curses depending upon infidelity and blessing upon fidelity to the covenant.

Treaties in this form were used by the princes of the so-called New Empire of the Hittites. After that they seem to disappear from common use, so that Mendenhall can claim that if the Mosaic covenant reflects this pattern, it must go back to a time contemporaneous with the Hittite Empire, which came to an end in the last years of the thirteenth century B.C. He points out that it is not unreasonable to compare Hittite and Israelite materials; there are certain evidences of contact between the two peoples (p. 28).[3]

The historical reconstruction based on this evidence is plausible and enticing. Still, there have been warning voices. The whole structure is based on one support, the apparent formal similarity between the ancient oriental treaty and the O.T. covenant, especially the Decalogue. This is a narrow base in-

the *vassal treaty*, a pact imposed by an overlord on a more or less willing vassal: there are also *parity treaties*, pacts between princes of equal status whether 'Great Kings' or princes of lesser rank (treaties of the latter sort are in evidence at Alalakh): formally the two kinds are the same. Some further definitions may be in order; this study uses *covenant* for any agreement or compact binding persons together: *treaty* means a compact between nations: *treaty form* means such a compact expressed in the fashion of the outline given in the text: *covenant form* is the same, but this designation is reserved to such instances as may be used to express Israel's relation to its God.

A much-to-be-desired new edition of the treaty texts themselves by E. von Schuler is promised as vol. 1 of *Die Staatsverträge des Altertums*, ed. H. Bengtson. Vol. 2, H. Bengtson, *Die Verträge der griechisch-römischen Welt von 700 bis 338 v. Chr.*, München, 1962, has already appeared.

[3] Now H. Otten, '*Ein kanaanäischer Mythus im Hethitischem*', MIO 1, 125 ff.: C. Rabin, 'Hittite Words in Hebrew', *Or* n.s. 32 (1963), 113–39, are to be added to Mendenhall's references.

deed, and it is possible to arrive at roughly similar conclusions from different premises.[4] Even some who accept the validity of the formal comparison of treaty and covenant warn us against hasty historical conclusions.[5]

The amphictyony concept, for example, plays a considerable role in Mendenhall's historical reconstruction. In his view the tribes were originally united only by their covenanted relation to Yahweh, that is, through a form of amphictyony. The position becomes difficult if the amphictyony analogy becomes doubtful, and, as we have seen, recent studies have raised doubts about it.

So, though they have won an acceptance so wide that one can speak of a consensus,[6] Mendenhall's historical views have not remained uncriticized. The same is to be said of his analysis of literary forms; the debate demands further investigation.

Treaty Texts and Covenant Texts

According to Mendenhall the Decalogue as it appears in Exodus and Deuteronomy is to be taken as part of a treaty-like covenant between Yahweh and Israel (pp. 35–41). The Decalogue opens with the assertion: 'I am Yahweh, your God, who brought you out of Egypt.' Here we have the equivalent of the preamble, the introduction of the sovereign who is making the covenant, and it is also the historical prologue. The sovereign is here identified by his intervention in the history of the people with whom he is dealing, and his claim to their allegiance is established or at least reinforced by the reference to his generosity in history. Then there is the immediate transition to the expression of the sovereign's will which is expressed less in matters of detail than in fundamental principles. This identification of the Decalogue with the treaty form through the sequence: preamble—historical prologue plus basic law, has been widely accepted.[7] Nonetheless,

---

[4] Masao Sekine, 'Davidsbund und Sinaibund bei Jeremia', *Vetus Testamentum* 9 (1959), 47–57.

[5] J. A. Thompson, 'The Near Eastern Suzerain-Vassal Concept in the Religion of Israel', *The Journal of Religious History* 3 (1964), 1–19.

[6] So F. L. Moriarty, S.J., 'Prophet and Covenant', *Gregorianum* 66 (1965), 817.

[7] Perhaps this influenced Mowinckel, *The Psalms in Israel's Worship*, Nashville, 1962, vol. 1, 180, to change his earlier opinion that the law was an entrance liturgy and accept it as intrinsic to the covenant cult: D. N. Freedman, 'Divine Commitment and Human Obligation', *Interpretation*

it is not without its problems, as we shall see after completing the
survey of the views of Mendenhall and those who follow his ideas.

Mendenhall himself seeks the various elements of the treaty
form scattered through various O.T. texts, where they are taken
to be relics of the originally complete form. Thus Jos. 24:25–7
gives us references to further 'statutes and laws, witnesses, and
some kind of document'. If it is difficult to find any reference to
the essential curses and blessings in Exodus or Joshua, we know
from a book like Deuteronomy that Israel did know a form of
covenant in which curses and blessings were connected with the
stipulations.

Despite many difficulties in detail, the evidence that Israel
uses the treaty-form in some, at least, of its religious literature,
and uses it to describe its special relationship with Yahweh, is
irrefragable. There is not another literary form from among those
of the ancient Near East which is more certainly evident in the
Old Testament.[8] The question is, just where and at what stage
of the tradition it is to be found.

It is, then, understandable that Mendenhall's views have been
integrated into other studies of the Old Testament. One aspect of
this has been a certain apologetic use of the idea, a use which
does not, indeed, seem to have been far from the mind of Prof.
Mendenhall himself. Thus, William Moran has tried to show in
more detail the correspondence between the Mosaic covenant and
the Hittite treaty-form. He seeks to answer some of the objections
to the existence of such a correspondence, such as the problem
that there is no placing of the covenant document in a shrine (he
points out that the document was traditionally contained in the
Ark of the Covenant which was, if not a shrine, certainly an
extremely holy object).[9] Further, the ideas of Mendenhall are

18 (1964), 419–31: A. Kapelrud, 'Some Recent Points of View on the
Time and Origin of the Decalogue', *Studia theologica* 18 (1964), 81–90:
and P. Buis, *Le Deutéronome. Sources bibliques*, Paris, 1963, 13, 61–2, all
accept the basic identification, surely sufficient evidence for its widespread
appeal.

[8] Accepted, for instance, by W. Zimmerli, *The Law and the Prophets*,
Oxford, 1965, 52–60, and 'Das Gesetz im Alten Testament', *Gottes
Offenbarung. Theologische Bucherei* 19, Munich, 1963, 268: and G. von
Rad, *Deuteronomy*, London, 1966, 21–2.

[9] 'Moses und der Bundesschluss am Sinai', *Stimmen der Zeit* 170 (1961–
62), 120–33: in Latin in *Verbum Domini* 40 (1962), 3–17.

basic to the view of Israel's history which governs the well-known *History of Israel* by John Bright.

Besides these investigations of larger literary and historical problems there have been studies of detailed correspondences between treaty and covenant. A remarkable instance has been pointed out by Moran, who shows that the omnipresent Deuteronomic word love (*'ahab*) is borrowed directly from the treaty tradition and appears in Deuteronomy with a meaning which is exactly that of the 'love' which the vassal owed his overlord. The vassal was called upon to be faithful, to dedicate himself to the service of his overlord. This is a 'love' which is essentially obedience and fidelity, a love which could be and was commanded.[10] N. Lohfink, following upon Moran, has shown that Hosea 9:15 reflects this usage, even though the normal and very frequent use of 'love' in Hosea is quite different.[11] Further, following on Moran's discovery that Akkadian *ṭubtu*, 'goodness, 'friendship' is technical treaty terminology, D. Hillers has found parallel use of the Hebrew cognate *ṭôbah* in Deut. 23:4–7 and 2 Sam. 2:6, and 1 Kgs. 12:7 shows the same usage according to A. Malamat.[12]

Criticism of the Form-Critical Parallel: Treaty and Covenant

We have already noted some of the cautions raised against the too ready acceptance of the covenant-treaty parallel, particularly in regard to the historical conclusions attached to it. It should not be forgotten that there have been more general caveats raised by scholars of stature. Precisely because the form-critical parallel has been so widely accepted and because it seems to be borne out by the detailed correspondences just mentioned

[10] 'The Ancient Near Eastern Background of the Love of God in Deuteronomy', *CBQ* 25 (1963), 77–87.

[11] 'Hate and Love in Osee 9;15', *CBQ* 25 (1963), 417. F. C. Fensham has devoted a number of studies to parallels in detail between the treaties and the Old Testament: 'Clauses of protection in Hittite Treaties and in the Old Testament', *VT* 13 (1963), 133–43; 'Maledictions and Benedictions in Ancient Near Eastern Vassal-Treaties and the Old Testament', *ZAW* 74 (1962), 1–9; 'Salt and Curse in the Old Testament and the Ancient Near East', *BA* 25 (1962), 48–50.

[12] W. L. Moran, S.J., 'A Note on the Treaty Terminology of the Sefire Stelas', *JNES* 22 (1963), 173–6: D. Hillers, 'A Note on Some Treaty Terminology in the Old Testament', *BASOR* 176 (1964), 46–7: A. Malamat, 'Organs of Statecraft in the Israelite Monarchy', *BA* 28 (1965), 34–65.

it is good to give some attention to these before continuing the
discussion of further form-critical and other studies. If one fails
to take any notice of the problems until he has seen the mass of
positive reactions and the work which follows from them, he will
almost certainly get a distorted picture of the actual state of
affairs in Old Testament scholarship. So much material gives
an impression of unanimity which is far from being the true state
of things.

In fact important works have considered the analogy of the Old
Testament covenant between God and Israel with the treaty and
have found it wanting. For instance, H. J. Kraus, studying the
treaty analogy in relation to Israel's worship, concludes that it
may well obscure or even distort the true Old Testament concept
of covenant. He does not deny that a text like Joshua 24 has
elements which bear a close external resemblance to the make-up
of the ancient treaties. However, he finds that there is in-
sufficient evidence for a true correspondence between the treaty
form and the Israelite covenant.

If anything, there is perhaps evidence for some sort of ritual in
Israel which followed a sequence rather like that of the ancient
Hittite treaty: introduction of God, historical prologue, and the
rest, but this is not to say that we have a covenant form, an actual
contractual form of the covenant relationship.[13] This judgment
is similar to that of J. J. Stamm in his second edition of the survey of recent thought concerning the Decalogue. He also holds
that the covenant itself does not seem to have been described and
expressed according to this form, but that there is an analogy
between the sequence of events of the Israelite ritual and of the
parts of the Hittite treaty.[14] It should be noted that experts agree
that the treaties themselves, the extra-biblical documents, actually
came into force only when the proper ceremonies were per-
formed and they may well reflect elements of this ritual.

[13] H. J. Kraus, *Worship in Israel*, Oxford, 1966, 136–40.
[14] J. J. Stamm and M. E. Andrew, *The Ten Commandments in Recent
Research*, Studies in Biblical Theology 2/2, 42–3. H. Graf Reventlow, 'Kultisches Recht im Alten Testament', *Zeitschrift für Theologie und Kirche*
60 (1963), 267–304, believes that there is a parallel between treaty and
covenant, but that Israel did not borrow the treaty form for its religious
purposes (276): rather both treaty and the covenant-related apodictic law
were essentially cultic and perhaps different, parallel developments from
a single ritual source (278–80).

Martin Noth has pointed out some further problems. For one, he sees (correctly, it seems to me) a tendency to treat the treaty-covenant formula as a kind of absolute, independent of its literary-critical and traditio-historical contexts. This is to abuse form-critical methodology. Further, he has some wise words regarding the use of the treaty analogy to build or fortify historical theories. He asks what is gained by establishing—even if one could do so in this way—the 'bare fact' of this or that historical point in regard to the patriarchs or to Moses or whatever. What is of ultimate importance in any primary text such as the Bible is to study the traditions as it offers them to us in their entire complexity.[15]

The importance of this call for precision and concern for context in studies of the covenant and the treaties may be illustrated from the problem of the Decalogue. It is often treated as the text of a treaty in full form between Yahweh and Israel. Then, sometimes as a reason for so doing, sometimes as a result of it, the treaty is taken to be the source of the apodictic type of law ('Thou shalt (not)'), which, while not exclusive to Israel, is characteristic of Israelite law.

But is the Decalogue a text in treaty form or at least the remains of one? Apart from the entire lack of the essential element of curses or blessings conditioned by obedience to the law, to be discussed further on in this study, the resemblance to the treaty form is far from perfect. Typically the treaty begins thus: 'These are the words of the Sun, Mursilis, the Great King, the king of Hatti . . .'. The opening words of Deuteronomy: 'These are the words which Moses spoke . . .' are the Hebrew equivalent of this.[16] The first sentence of the Decalogue lacks the characteristic 'These are the words of' and the speaker begins in the first person without any quotation formula parallel to 'These are the words of . . .'. Further, if the clause 'who brought you out of Egypt' is to be equated with anything in the opening formula of the treaties, it should be the identification of the sovereign: 'Great King, king of X', for this is what normally follows the name of the sovereign. Only after the identifying titles does the

---

[15] M. Noth, *Developing Lines of Theological Thought in Germany*, *Annual Bibliographical Lecture* 4, Richmond, Va., 1963.
[16] First noted by M. G. Kline, 'Dynastic Covenant', *Westminster Theological Journal* 23 (1961).

history begin, and that absolutely, not as a clause subordinate to the opening words like the relative clause of the Decalogue.[17]

As for the treaty origins of the apodictic form of law, there is no doubt that some of the treaties have long sequences of apodictic commands. Externally at least these might be models for the collections of apodictic law such as we have in the Decalogue and elsewhere in the Old Testament. However, E. Gerstenberger has questioned whether this is the fact, and with good reasons. He shows that the more extensive accumulations of apodictic laws in the O.T. are secondary. The original appearances of the form did not have as many as ten members but perhaps only two or three, and the collections in which ten or twelve apodictic laws are taken together are a later development. Further, he shows that these apodictic laws had a very close affinity to the maxims. This connection with the Wisdom tradition enables him to trace the origins of apodictic law to the traditional wisdom of the clan or family, handed down from elder to younger in single maxims or at most in small sets usually of two or three members.[18]

F. Nötscher made a more general attack upon the comparison of the treaties with the Old Testament covenant.[19] Apart from its

---

[17] Problems like these concerning the identification of the Decalogue do not mean that one must deny its great antiquity. A Mosaic dating of the Commandments has been argued on other grounds; cf. H. H. Rowley, 'Moses and the Decalogue', *Men of God: Studies in Old Testament History and Prophecy*, London, 1963, 1–36, and J. P. Hyatt, 'Moses and the Ethical Decalogue', *Encounter* 26 (1965), 199–206.

[18] E. Gerstenberger, *Wesen und Herkunft des 'apodiktischen Rechts'*, *WMANT* 20, Neukirchen, 1965: 'Covenant and Commandment', *JBL* 84 (1965), 38–51. Earlier B. Gemser, 'The Importance of the Motive Clause in Old Testament Law', *VT Suppl.* 1 (1953), 50–66, recognized the importance of the Wisdom tradition in the growth of Israelite Law, and recently J. Malfroy, 'Sagesse et loi dans le Deutéronome', *VT* 15 (1965), 49–65, has shown that this tradition strongly influenced the Deuteronomic school. K. Koch, *The Growth of the Biblical Tradition*, New York, 1968, although he recognizes the purely external parallel between some stipulations of the Hittite treaties and the apodictic laws, believes that the Decalogue, the prime example of such laws, cannot be earlier than the monarchy, and he receives Gerstenberger's ideas with sympathy.

[19] F. Nötscher, 'Bundesformular und "Amtsschimmel",' *Biblische Zeitschrift* 9 (1965), 181–24. A detailed critique of this article in the German edition of this book has been condensed here, since it would seem to be of little interest to the English reader and is available to the scholar in the German.

repetition of Noth's useful warnings against over-hasty historical conclusions and careless literary-critical study, it has little of value to offer. It fails to distinguish the very different directions such comparative work has taken. It repeats points already made. It rejects the place of the cult in forming and preserving the traditions of the Old Testament. It underestimates badly the length of time a literary form can remain alive. Perhaps worst of all it cannot accept the possibility that a foreign, 'secular' form could be used to express Israel's relation to its God. It is doubtless true that this relation was special, but it could only be expressed in human terms. This means that man could speak of it only haltingly, using the analogy of the one thing he knows directly, his daily, secular experience.

The Sinai Covenant and Shechem

Since Mendenhall's work, which covered a great deal of ground in short compass, we have had a number of studies of particular texts or groups of texts. W. Beyerlin has made a detailed study of the traditions concerning the events at Sinai in which he asserts the correspondence between the Decalogue and the Hittite treaty-form. He recognizes that there are many lacunae in these correspondences; for instance, the Decalogue lacks the essential curse and blessing formula of the treaties. He claims that the apodictic form of the Decalogue implies curse and blessing, and so equivalently the document has this form. The Decalogue, with its designation of Yahweh as the God of the Exodus, is thus ancient and an essential part of the Sinai complex. In this way one of the most striking propositions of modern scholarship, von Rad's hypothesis that the Sinai traditions and the Exodus traditions were originally separate, can be denied. The Exodus would be the historical event, the subject of narrative, while the happenings at Sinai would rather be the acts in which the covenant between Yahweh and his people was formalized and given external expression. One is material for narrative, the other is an action, probably a ritual action. The ritual action would include as part of its *hieros logos* the presentation of Yahweh as the Lord of Israel's history who had guided Israel out of Egypt, and the connection between Sinai and the Exodus would be primal, Sinai the event, Exodus the history there recited.[20]

[20] *Origins and History of the Oldest Sinaitic Traditions*, Oxford, 1965.

Whatever may be the case with the original link between the Exodus and Sinai (and it would seem that the burden of proof still lies on those who would separate what the text of Exodus connects), it is hardly possible to accept this argument for the treaty character of the Decalogue. We have already seen some of the difficulties with this idea when the text is examined in detail. In recognizing the need for something like the conditional curses and blessings, Beyerlin has put his finger on a major problem, for they are a truly essential element in the treaty form. However, even though apodictic law implies sanctions as all law does, it does not state them, and it is the *statement* of them in the form of curses or blessings which cha acterizes the treaty as a literary form. From this point of view case law is closer to the treaty because it does state a penalty. This is not to claim that law had anything to do with the treaty as such. It is simply to point out that an argument from the implications of a given form for stating laws does nothing to show a connection with the treaty form.

Another study based on the traditio-historical possibilities of the treaty form has been devoted to Josh. 24. In it J. L'Hour tries to reconstruct the original form of the covenant believed to have been promulgated at Shechem.[21] In broad outline, his hypothesis is that the present text of Josh. 24 presents relics of a covenant in treaty form. There is an historical prologue, there are oaths and witnesses. However, the stipulations, the detailed laws, of this covenant have been displaced. Only the statement that Joshua gave laws and statutes to Israel remains (Josh. 24:26), but this is enough to show that there were such stipulations originally. These would be more or less the laws which we find now in the Covenant Code in Exodus. They will have been moved into the Sinai context in order to avoid naming anyone but Moses as giver or mediator of divine law. If we combine these laws with what remains in Josh. 24 and accept Exod. 23:20–33,

Thus he reaffirms on a new basis the position of his teacher, A. Weiser, *Introduction to the Old Testament*, London, 1961, 81–99. Similar arguments will be found in H. B. Huffmon, 'The Exodus, Sinai and the Credo', *CBQ* 27 (1965), 101–13, and more completely in R. E. Clements, *Prophecy and Covenant, Studies in Biblical Theology* 43, London, 1965, but without the peculiar claim about the nature of the Decalogue. H. Wildberger, *Jahwes Eigentumsvolk, ATANT* 37, Zurich, 1960, 69–73, still maintains the original separation of the Exodus and Sinai traditions.

[21] 'L'Alliance de Sichem', *RB* 69 (1962), 5–36, 161–84, 350–68.

as a sufficient blessing formula, we have a complete treaty form. However, the promise at the end of Exod. 23 looks more like a guarantee for the journey to the promised land than an authentic treaty- or covenant-conditioned blessing. In any case the whole reconstruction remains hypothetical in the highest degree, especially in view of the problems with the view of early Israel as a covenanted amphictyony which we have already seen. If this view is itself an uncertain theory, then the description of the form of the covenant on which the amphictyony was based is an hypothesis built upon another hypothesis. We are a long way from the texts themselves.

Conquest and Temple

Mendenhall himself has proposed an historical reconstruction which is related to his theories as to the covenant. According to this, the original Israel was no tribal unity at all. It was a gathering of refugees and rebels around the covenant God. Thus the picture of the conquest as given in the biblical books is a construct, an affirmation of tribal unity in accord with the mentality of the time, but the reality was something quite different. The covenanted God of Israel offered a rallying point for the poor and the oppressed of the time. But these poor and oppressed were not so much slaves in Egypt as the oppressed peasant population of Palestine itself. We know that late Bronze Age Canaanite society did have an overbearing aristocracy which lived off the labours of the peasant population. When the preachers of Yahwism appeared, they offered a rallying point for this population and revolt came. Essentially the conquest was not the taking over of the land by tribes entering from the desert, and Israel did not have significant nomadic or semi-nomadic antecedents. Israel was formed by the rebellious peasants of Canaan itself who entered into a treaty-covenant relationship with Yahweh. In connection with this, Mendenhall claims that any new structuring of society which comes close to reproducing the ancient Canaanite with its princes and with upper and lower classes would be a deviation from the original revolutionary Yahwist norm. Thus the kingship brings great danger of apostasy to the Hebrews, and is exceedingly hard to reconcile with the true Mosaic covenant.[22]

[22] G. Mendenhall, 'The Hebrew Conquest of Palestine', *BA* 35 (1962), 66–87.

This reconstruction is interesting but hardly successful. There is simply too much evidence which makes the Hebrews, before their entrance into Palestine, something like nomads: the patriarchs are presented, for instance, as essentially semi-nomadic shepherds.[23] And it seems to me impossible to deny a major role to some *groups* who did indeed experience God's salvation in Egypt and brought the message to Palestine. The work of Alt and Noth has long since shown us that not all the Hebrews came into Palestine under Moses and Joshua, that many were already settled there, and that many strangers joined the original Yahwist tribe, but still the nomadic element and the element of movement from Egypt must be retained as a major aspect of ancient Israelite history.

Deuteronomy is essential to any study of the later development of Israelite religion, and, since it is pre-eminently a covenant document, it is impossible to dissociate this study from the new interest in covenant. One aspect of this is the problem of the origin of the book. It has been the common opinion that the primitive book (*Urdeuteronomium*, the law code with, almost certainly, the introduction in chapters (5) 6–11 and the conclusion in chapter 28) was the document discovered in the Temple under Josiah and that it was of northern (Samarian) origin. Without denying the first of these opinions, important studies have questioned the second.

R. E. Clements has argued that the book is from Jerusalem. He bases his case on the Deuteronomic insistence on a unique sanctuary, an insistence he traces to the influence of the Temple. Further, he finds that the favourite Deuteronomic word *baḥar*, 'choose, elect', is borrowed from the royal ideology of Jerusalem, that the claim that the ark of the covenant is a mere container is a polemic against the Jerusalite idea that it was Yahweh's footstool, and that the anti-Canaanite bias of Deuteronomy is really directed against the Canaanite influence on the ritual of the Temple. Such rebellious ideas could, he thinks, have arisen only

---

[23] Denied in W. F. Albright, *The Biblical Period from Abraham to Ezra*, New York, 1963, 5–9, but see R. De Vaux, O.P., 'The Hebrew Patriarchs and History', *Theology Digest* 12 (1964), 235–6. P. Buis and J. Leclercq, *Le Deutéronome. Sources bibliques*, Paris, 1963, 13, hold that the 'covenant in Moab' (Deut. 29–30) was a real uniting of nomadic groups in preparation for the conquest of Palestine.

in Jerusalem, as a reaction of those zealous for the covenant reli-gion of Yahweh against foreign concepts.[24] In fact, some of these ideas were or became essential to the covenant concept. One is the idea of election. Then the centrality of worship, because it was felt to be essential to undivided allegiance to Yahweh, is linked to the basic covenant precept.

N. Lohfink has studied the problem of the origin of Deutero-nomy with explicit attention to the covenant form.[25] He points out that the form would help explain the events and the reactions of the people. The problem is famous: Why was the document accepted as new and yet binding to the extent that men were terrorized by their failure to have lived according to it? The mere fact of coming from the Temple or of having conditioned curses appended hardly explain this. (As to the latter: the men of Judah had stood up remarkably well to the threats of the prophets. Why should these threats have special effect?) If we assume that the document was in the covenant form, some of these difficulties are easier to answer. Since covenant was at the heart of their religion, the Hebrews would have recognized that this *kind* of thing was binding. The very fact of coming from the Temple would correspond to the familiar document clause.

These arguments have varying weight. If this kind of covenant was familiar to all Hebrews of the time—which is not proven—would it not be accepted even though of northern origin? Or might not the refugees from Samaria in a hundred years of residence in Judah have made their ideas familiar enough to be accepted as authoritative from such a source? Finally, it is im-possible to establish that the document clause calling for preser-vation of the treaty or covenant document was peculiar to or even a usual part of the form. Hence it could not be the basis for the respect shown the Temple document. On the other hand, recent history had made the treaty a familiar enough form, since the Assyrians used it regularly. Further, it was well known what terrible punishments violation of an Assyrian treaty called down upon the violator. Hence its general resemblance to the treaties would make Deuteronomy just the sort of document which would fit the events described in 2 Kgs. 22.

[24] 'Deuteronomy and the Jerusalem Cult-Tradition', *VT* 15 (1965), 300–15.
[25] 'Die Bundesurkunde des Königs Josias', *Biblica* 44 (1963), 461–98.

Form-Critical Studies of a Larger Range of Texts

We turn now to studies which represent independent investigations. They constitute a control of the comparison between
treaty and covenant on the basis of a larger number of biblical
texts as well as the extra-biblical materials.

The first of these is the work of K. Baltzer.[26]

Once again he presents the structure of the Hittite vassal treaty
and then seeks analogies to it in the O.T. literature. He finds that
some additions or precisions in detail have to be added to the
analysis of the treaty form. Thus he points out that the treaties
often contained a description of boundaries, and he tends to take
certain geographical elements in O.T. texts relating to the
covenant as separate elements in the formal structure of the
covenant (pp. 22, 30, 46). Perhaps more significantly, he notes
that the treaties have after the historical prologue a *Grundsatzerklärung* before they turn to the detailed stipulations. Again he
finds this declaration of principle very much an element in the
covenant form in the O.T. (pp. 22-3, 31, 37-8, etc.). Baltzer
discusses at some length the important text, Josh. 24, one of the
bases of Mendenhall's theory, and finds there elements of the
covenant form, although his analysis differs in many details from
Mendenhall's. On the other hand, he is much more reluctant to
get involved in the details of the covenant as depicted at Sinai.
He refuses to begin with the pericope and he points out that the
literary-critical problems of these texts make it extremely difficult
to discern the formal elements, although he does point out that
certain elements which also appear in the treaties will certainly
be found in the Sinai pericope (pp. 37-40). In addition to this,
Baltzer points out elements of the treaty form of the covenant,
such as historical deeds used to base a claim on obedience,
threats or blessings and so on, which are characteristic of the
treaty, and which do recur in the Old Testament frequently. He
thus carries the argument further than Mendenhall, and shows
the pervasiveness of elements which resemble those of the treaty
form. At the same time, he is very reluctant to make historical

---

[26] *Das Bundesformular*, *WMANT* 4, Neukirchen, 1960. The references
in the text are to this edition. The reprint of 1964 is unchanged except for
a short bibliography added at the beginning of the book. (ET in preparation, Oxford, 1971.)

conclusions on the basis of literary form in the manner of Mendenhall. He warns against hasty historical conclusions (p. 17, n. 6), and he himself is concerned primarily with the literary phenomena and their milieu, their *Sitz im Leben*. In this latter regard, Baltzer has a valuable discussion of the evidence for the ceremonial renewal of the covenant between Yahweh and his people and the circumstances in which these renewals were carried out (47–70). This occurred when, for one reason or another, it was felt that the covenant had been broken. An obvious sign of this was the actuation of the curses. When plagues and troubles came upon the people, they knew that they had been faithless, and that God was punishing their infidelity. A prophet might also warn the people that they had violated the covenant.

Also valuable is the study of the reaffirmation (*Bestätigung*) of the covenant and its circumstances (pp. 71–90). The Israelites seem to have felt that the covenant had to be reaffirmed when an important change in leadership occurred. There is evidence of this when Joshua succeeded Moses (Deut. 31–Josh. 1), when Joshua was about to die (Josh. 23), when Samuel instituted the monarchy (1 Sam. 12). Note that this does not always mean that the death of the old leader is at hand, as the instance of Samuel and the monarchy shows. In addition to what Baltzer has to say about the circumstances of this reaffirmation of covenant, we might note that this was often (even normally?) accompanied by a theophany (Deut. 31; 1 Sam. 12; 1 Kgs. 8). Note that this reaffirmation of the covenant seems not to have been required at every change, whether of ruler or of something else (p. 64). This is clear from treaty procedure also, since treaties like the Aramaic text from Sefire and Esarhaddon's pact with his vassals explicitly bind not only the man who makes the treaty but his successors. It has been suggested that such reaffirmation was required in Israel only when a dynasty changed. Thus the covenant between God, king and people was reaffirmed when the Davidid Joash succeeded the usurper Athaliah.[27]

My own study re-assesses the evidence from the Hittite treaties and adds the data from a number of texts which are treaties but are not Hittite, so as to integrate the treaties into their

[27] A. Malamat, 'Organs of Statecraft in the Israelite Monarchy', *BA* 28 (1965), 36–37.

background in ancient Near Eastern legal practice.[28] All admit that the basic legal idea of the contract in the treaties used by the Hittites is of Mesopotamian origin. In addition to what was known in the past, there is evidence that some form of treaty relationship was much in use among the peoples known to us through the archives of Mari, and the tablets from Alalakh have shown us that treaties were in use in Syria at a very early age, the eighteenth century, as well as in the fifteenth and fourteenth centuries when Hittite influence was important. There are also treaties from the post-Hittite period, treaties involving peoples of Syria and Mesopotamia, especially the Assyrians, and these take us down into the seventh century B.C. It would seem that the same legal-literary form, essentially stipulations sanctioned by oath, was used to express these treaty relationships all through two millennia of ancient Near Eastern history.

There are characteristics peculiar to each period, particularly among the Hittites the use of the historical prologue, and among the Syrians and Mesopotamians the tremendous emphasis upon the curses. However, the historical prologue, while characteristic of the Hittites, does not seem to have been peculiar to them; it appears in the eighteenth-century B.C. treaty from Alalakh. Moreover, it is not indispensable in the Hittite treaty; there are a number of examples of Hittite treaties which do lack the historical introduction.[29] Further, the document-clause, that is, the

---

[28] D. J. McCarthy, S.J., *Treaty and Covenant. A Study in Form in the Ancient Oriental Documents and in the Old Testament, Analecta Biblica* 21, Rome, 1963.

[29] Ibid., 30–1: denied by H. B. Huffmon, *CBQ* 27 (1965), 109, n. 41, because he believes that the treaties between Mursilis II and Niqmepa of Ugarit and between Suppliuliumas I and Huqqanas have historical prologues. However, what he calls historical prologues merely affirm that the Hittite king has made these men kings: he is the legal source of their power. This is more a question of legal than of historical fact, since there was an extensive history of Hittite-Ugaritic relations which a normal historical prologue would have to have included. Why should the history be suppressed here if it is indispensable? Even an edict involving Ugarit and Hatti, RS 17.340 (J. Nougayrol, *Palais royale d'Ugarit*, Paris, 1956, IV, 48–52) has its historical element. (This text might be called a treaty, but there are problems with it; not, as Huffmon. op. cit., 105, n. 20, implies, merely because it is unilateral, but rather because it lacks any sign of an oath: further, the lack of reference to a treaty tying Ugarit to Hatti in other international agreements involving Ugarit and other states (not merely in later treaties with Hatti) is a very telling point indeed, since

command to guard the treaty texts carefully and to reread it regularly, is very rarely found in the treaties—so rarely that it is difficult to see how it can be legitimately claimed as a necessary part of the form (pp. 38–9). In any event, it has always been known that this demand for a written document was not native

the evidence from contemporary Alalakh shows that the suzerain's demand to control the external affairs of vassals was respected in agreements between a vassal and other princes, and this in matters relating to fugitives, etc., things which are the subject of many international accords from the Ugaritic archives. Because it is a supplementary document Huffmon suspects the treaty character of the Abba-AN text from Alalakh (ibid., 104, n. 18), even though it is clearly a sworn contract between princes, i.e., the very definition of a treaty: the suspicions surely should be stronger in respect to RS 17.340.) The Huqqanas treaty also, if it had a normal historical prologue, would develop the personal relations of the vassal with Hittite royalty as, e.g., in the Kupanta-KAL and Manapa-Dattas treaties. Further, Huffmon asserts that the Ulmi-Teshub treaty has an initial lacuna which might have held an historical prologue, but the traces remaining do not leave enough space for a normal prologue. As for the fragmentary treaty with Piyassilis of Carchemish, the Hittite version of the Aziru treaty (H. Freydank, *Mitteilungen des Instituts für Orientforschung* 7 (1960), 356–81) does indeed affect the argument since it shows that the sovereign's demands can begin ahead of the history: hence it is possible that the missing parts of the Piyassilis treaty might have held a historical section. But if we are to be logical we have equally to admit that this opens the possibility that the fragmentary Zidantas-Pilliya treaty had its history and not, with Huffmon, separate the two similar instances and allow no history in the latter treaty only. Since the oldest Hittite documents have their 'historical prologues', the age of this last treaty is no argument for its not having one. In any case, we must note the character of the demands which precede the history in the Hittite Aziru treaty; they lay down the basic demands of vassal loyalty and tribute. These, a kind of *Grundsatzerklärung*, can thus appear without an historical foundation and justification. In other words, the juridical basis for the treaty relationship can be something other than the historic relationship of the parties. This leaves the major point open; the Hittite treaty was a flexible legal and literary form and a historical relationship is no indispensable basis for the relationship it set up. In particular the treaty with Piyassilis does not have a *Grundsatzerklärung* immediately after the opening titulature: it deals with succession to the throne and special honours (*tuḫkantis*) reserved to the royal family, privileges which a ceremonious society would normally wish to see explicitly connected with past rights: even the reverse of the tablet continues with the same sort of thing (the privilege of remaining seated before the Great King: see H. Otten, *ZA* n.f. 16 (1958), 234–5). Hence the absence of a history in the prominent opening position still seems strange.

Hittite but was adopted from Mesopotamian legal practice. Another important point: there is another type of treaty, the parity treaty between princes of equal status. Although the relationship set up by this kind of treaty was very different from that produced by the vassal treaty, formally the two types of treaties are identical.

If the historical prologue was not an essential element and if it appears outside of Hatti in a treaty from Alalakh,[30] we must be careful in using the appearance of the form for historical dating. Indeed, scholars will always be wary of using literary forms to argue to historical dates, since literary forms can and do have a complex and variable history, and we can judge little about the effects of time in terms of change and alteration. Furthermore, literary forms, if they are what they are claimed to be, namely, expressions arising from given social circumstances, may well be the product of similar circumstances in different times and different places, without there necessarily being an historical connection among the different appearances.[31]

This is by no means to deny that the covenant form does appear in the Old Testament. However, we must proceed with caution and careful attention to detail and to variations. To take the clearest example, there can be no doubt that Deuteronomy does show some kind of relationship to the literary forms of these treaties. It has the same sequence: historical material, stipulations, curses and blessings.[32] Moreover, certain self-contained

[30] See D. J. Wiseman, 'Abban and Alalakh', *JCS* 12 (1958), 124–9, for the example: discussed in McCarthy, op. cit., 57–9, where it is pointed out that the historical element seems to be a development of a legal form, the description of the antecedent circumstances of a case. We may add a somewhat similar example from Ugarit, RS 19.68, lines 5–10 (J. Nougayrol, *Palais royale d'Ugarit*, Paris, 1956, IV, 284), with their delicate reference to the past disagreements between Ugarit and Amurru which the treaty text RS 19.68 is to settle (among other things).

[31] R. Smend, *Die Bundesformel*, Theologische Studien 68, Zürich, 1963, 34 with n. 16, claims that this is in fact the case with the formula, 'Yahweh the God of Israel, Israel the people of Yahweh'; very similar formulae appear in treaties in the nature of the case, not because of any cross-influence.

[32] This is true in the first instance of the central core, Deut. 5–28 (cf. McCarthy, *Treaty and Covenant*, 109-30: M. Kline, 'Dynastic Covenant', *Westminster Theological Journal* 23 (1960/61), 1 ff., argues that the whole book, as it stands in the present text of the Bible, is a unity on the basis

units in the so-called framework to Deuteronomy, chapters 4 and 29–30, show a similarity to this structure, although they are cast as speeches. It would appear that the form was used as a model for speech-making.

The procedure involved here, that of comparing narratives or speeches with legal documents, has been questioned.[33] There may be a difficulty, but many (e.g., Mendenhall, Baltzer, et al.), rightly or wrongly interpret Josh. 24 in terms of the covenant form and seek to explain the absence of certain essential parts of that form. This would imply that they accept the possibility and the validity of the parallel. It is not in fact impossible that one type of literature imitates another; a classic example is Thucydides' using the structure of the Attic tragedy to build his history of the Peloponnesian War. Thus it is in the abstract possible that a narrative or speech follow the structure of the treaty form. In fact, we find that certain speeches follow the outline of the covenant form, so that the abstract possibility has been realized and it is reasonable to look for further examples. So also narrative and other sequences related to rites follow the outline (see above, nn. 28–30). After all this evidence it seems reasonable to question other texts in this regard. These other texts, it will be seen, are difficult. 1 Sam. 12 is quite close to the literary form, although there is little in the way of stipulation and the curse-blessing formula is distorted. Josh. 24, as has often been noted, does show elements from the form, but it is lacking a great number of important elements. If we are to affirm that it is a relic of this ancient literary form, we surely must explain the absence of such indispensable members of the form as the curse and blessing. Investigation of the events and the documents of Sinai (Exod. 19–34) seems to show little or nothing of the literary form of the covenant. There is simply no place in which the curses and blessings appear. There is, of course, the Decalogue with its apparent historical introduction, but this historical introduction here is almost certainly related to a theophany and serves to

of the covenant analogy, a thesis which he develops in *Treaty of the Great King*, Grand Rapids, 1963).

[33] H. B. Huffmon, *CBQ* 27 (1965), 104, n. 16: E. Gerstenberger, *JBL* 83 (1964), 199: F. Nötscher, *Biblische Zeitschrift* 9 (1965), 196. The view that Israelite preachers did use the covenant form is accepted and used by P. Buis and J. Leclercq, *Le Deutéronome*, 7, 17, 181.

identify the God who appears. Further, as was remarked above, the Decalogue itself is really something different from the apodictic stipulations of the treaties and can hardly be reduced to the treaty form.

It is certainly significant that, to say the least, the form is not at all clear in the basic covenant, that of Sinai, and that the texts in which it is clear are relatively late. The other texts in which at least elements of the form may with more or less probability be seen are also texts which have often been treated as late texts, i.e., connected with the Deuteronomic school or at least related to it stylistically. We need further and extensive investigation of the matter. It may be that the covenant form is connected with certain northern (i.e., Israelite as opposed to Judean) elements, while it is absent from southern sources.[34]

Covenant and Ritual

In any event, the covenant between Yahweh and Israel described in the Sinai narrative was a covenant based upon some sort of blood and sacrificial rite or, in another version (Exod. 24:11), a covenant meal[35] uniting Yahweh and the people, through which a quasi-familial relation was set up between the two. We cannot ignore the sacrificial and blood element in Exod. 24, the persistence of the tradition of a nexus between sacrifice and the covenant which is evidenced in Deut. 27, and the designation of a certain sort of sacrifice as a sacrifice of communion (*zebaḥ šelamîm*), that is to say, a sacrifice which produces a union between God and the people.[36] The evidence is overwhelming

[34] See Julien Harvey, *JBL* 84 (1965), 103: C. S. Whitley, *JNES* 22 (1963), 38, who suggests a connection between the Canaanite *ba'al bᵉrît* at Shechem and the traditions of covenant and covenant form which seem to centre around Shechem: N. Lohfink, *Das Hauptgebot, Analecta Biblica* 29, Rome, 1963, 176–80, has a brilliant exposition of the Gilgal covenant which seems to have affinities with the covenant form: see also J. Muilenburg, 'The Form and Structure of the Covenantal Formulation', *VT* (1959), 360–5, and H. Wildberger, *Jahwes Eigentumsvolk, ATANT* 37, Zürich/Stuttgart, 1960, 55–62, 65–8, on Gilgal.

[35] On the covenant meal see T. Gaster, *Thespis*,[2] New York, 1959, 372–5, with extensive references: E. Kutsch, *Salbung als Rechtsakt im AT und im alten Orient, BZAW* 87, Berlin, 1963, 19–20.

[36] On communion sacrifice, see R. de Vaux, O.P., *Studies in Old Testament Sacrifice*, Cardiff, 1964: also R. Schmid, *Das Bundesopfer in Israel, SANT* 9, Munich, 1964.

that there is a very strong cultic element in the most antique presentation of Israel's special relationship, its covenant relationship, with Yahweh. Covenant meal, sacrifice, and especially the overpowering experience of the theophany presented in the cult were certainly elements connected with and integral to the covenant. The God who appears in Sinai, a God appearing in cultic circumstances, as all agree, is such that his mere appearance founds the relationship between him and the people and supplies a sufficient ground for the demands he puts upon them.[37] What is important here is not the simple fact of emphasis on the rite in covenant-making but rather the contrast with the attitude of the treaties. These latter did indeed involve rites or at least a relation to cult, for instance, in the occasional demand that a copy be kept in a temple. In fact, they were based on an oath taken in a religious or cultic context. However, the emphasis is on the oath, the human act of taking on a solemn obligation, so much so that the very word for 'treaty' is taken from the oath in Akkadian, Hittite, and Aramaic, but not in ordinary Hebrew.[38]

Further Traces of the Covenant Form?

A. Weiser discovers the sequence of narrative and condemnation in Deut. 32:1–18, to be a ritual variation on the covenant form. This same sort of thing, a ritual reflecting the covenant form, is supposed to underlie 1 Sam. 10:17–26. He finds verse 18 to depend on the historical prologue and 19 the condemnation of Israel for breaking the covenant.[39]

There is a real danger in this sort of thing, as there is in the whole reassessment of the Israelite covenant with Yahweh which has been going on. The problem is in assuming that covenant is univocal, that all covenant in the Old Testament is of one kind,

[37] On the theophany see R. Smend, *Bundesformel*, 8, and the standard study of W. Zimmerli, 'Ich bin Jahwe', *Gottes Offenbarung*, 11–40.

[38] Surely a further indication that the ritual element is especially significant in the Israelite covenant, *contra* J. Scharbert, *Biblische Zeitschrift* 9 (1965), 291–2: it is not correct to say (ibid.) that the 'Blutriten von Ex. 24;5f sind ohne weiteres von den üblichen . . . Eidessitten des Alten Orients her zu verstehen', since the connection with sacrifice is singular and in any case the Old Testament attitude toward blood is specifically Israelite, not common to the ancient Orient (cf. L. Sirard, 'Sacrifices et rites sanglants dans l'Ancien Testament', *Sciences ecclésiastiques* 15 (1963), 192).   [39] A. Weiser, *Samuel*, *FRLANT* 81, Göttingen, 1962, 19.

the treaty form. Then anything which seems to be related to this form is treated as being covenantal. Such *a priori* reasoning must always be controlled by the study of each text as it is. This is not always the case.

For example, L. Alonso Schökel's fine study of the story of the fall in Gen. 2–3 asserts that there is a covenant element here simply because there is a commandment in Gen. 2:19.[40] Another example of the same thing will be found in W. R. Roehrs' article in which he assumes that all covenants in the Old Testament between God and Israel are of the same sort, that God is always the single active partner who grants the covenant, and that the covenant is the treaty form, even though he does not find that vassalship is basic.[41]

However, before we take the covenant form as a panacea for all our theological problems, we must establish an exact reference to the covenant form. If all covenant in the Old Testament is in the covenant form, well and good, we may proceed on this basis. However, if, as is the case (cf. the promissory covenant, for example), covenant is a very complex idea, and there are important elements of the O.T. which treat the covenant between Yahweh and his people as something very different from what is expressed in the covenant or treaty form, we must allow for this in our theology. As in so many other things, we are learning that our theology must be close to the text and carefully nuanced. Thus, another approach to the theology of law and covenant is enlightening. It points out that the covenant was also an affair of cult. It was therefore, something religious and not secular, not even legalistic and moralistic. The covenant was made, reaffirmed and renewed in the cult.[42]

Covenant and Family

Besides the cultic aspects of covenant there are important analogies other than the treaty analogy which are used to elucidate the covenant relationship between Yahweh and his people, the

[40] See 'Sapiential and Covenant Themes in the Old Testament', *Theology Digest* 13 (1965), 6–7 (=*Biblica* 43 (1962), 305 (in Spanish)).

[41] 'Covenant and Justification in the Old Testament', *Concordia Theological Monthly* 35 (1964), 583–602). A German version will be found in *Lutherischer Rundblick* 12 (1964), 154–72.

[42] See K. Baltzer, *Bundesformular*, 48–70: McCarthy, *Treaty and Covenant*, 152–67, 173–7.

marriage analogy and the father–son analogy. It is, of course, the prophet Hosea who introduces and develops the marriage analogy. Israel is the faithless wife of Yahweh, but Yahweh will not abandon her forever. After a period of chastisement she will be restored to her favoured position. And this idea is never lost sight of. In Jer. 31:32 Yahweh is described as acting as husband (*ba‘al*) toward Israel. In a recent discussion of the passage J. Coppens translates correctly: *J'ai dû sévir contre eux en époux.*[43] Thus Jeremiah carries on the image of the husband–wife relationship between Yahweh and Israel. Marriage, of course, like covenant, is a species of contractual relationship. Hence in this chapter of Jeremiah we are never far from the question of the covenant, an old covenant broken and the new covenant to be restored, but with new, affective overtones.

The father–son relationship is also a basic analogy for the relationship between Yahweh and Israel. This is not, of course, a contractual relationship in nature. However, Israel generally had no illusions that it was the literal, physical son of God. When it did think of itself as God's son, it was obviously in an adoptive sense.[44] Such an adoptive sense of the father–son relationship is essentially a contractual idea, and, as a matter of fact, the father–son relationship in the O.T. outside of one instance in Hosea and one in Deuteronomy, dependent upon Hosea, is described in terms which are identical with the terms which describe the covenant–love relationship between Yahweh and his people in the Deuteronomic theology. We have, then, an idea of father–son relationship which is essentially that of the covenant.[45] And there is no doubt that covenants, even treaties, were thought of as establishing a kind of quasi-familial unity. In the technical vocabulary of these documents a superior partner was called 'father', his inferior 'son', and equal partners were 'brothers'.

Covenant and Contract

We may conclude this survey of discussions of O.T. texts which are thought to be in one way or another direct reflections of the

---

[43] 'La nouvelle alliance en Jér 31. 31–4', *CBQ* 25 (1963), 14–15.
[44] See H. W. Wolff, *Hosea*, *BKAT* 14/1, Neukirchen, 1961, 255.
[45] See D. J. McCarthy, S.J., 'Notes on the Love of God in Deuteronomy and the Father–Son Relationship between Israel and Yahweh', *CBQ* 27 (1965), 144–7.

ancient treaty form with notice of the important precision contributed by G. Tucker.[46] He demonstrates that this form is not that of the contracts of the ancient Near East. Of course, a treaty or covenant must always be a contract in the generic sense of 'a binding agreement between two or more parties'. However, the manner of making and expressing this particular kind of agreement is not that of ordinary business contracts which (1) listed the parties, (2) described the transaction, (3) listed the witnesses to it, and (4) gave its date. In the contract, therefore, the basic agreement was not sworn under oath, although oaths about secondary matters could be included in the proceedings. In contrast to this, the treaty form is essentially a development of the ancient oath formula, i.e., a conditioned self-curse which would be activated if the oath were broken.[47]

[46] Gene M. Tucker, 'Covenant Forms and Contract Forms', *VT* 15 (1965), 487–503.

[47] As Tucker notes (p. 502), the formulae in Josh. 24:22; 'You are witnesses . . . We are witnesses', belong to the contract form. This is *not* a form of oath, a fact which further complicates the already difficult problem of Josh. 24, for it deprives that key text for the reconstruction of Israelite religious history on the basis of the covenant form of another of the essentials of that form.

3

Covenant and the Prophets

There has been an appeal to the covenant and the covenant form
in the effort to explain the prophets as well as the historical books.
It is not claimed that they used the covenant form itself. Rather
they were influenced by institutions and the forms of expression
characteristic of those institutions, and these reflect or at least
resemble the covenant form. Here three principal lines of argument have been followed: the connection of prophecy with
the celebration of the covenant in the cult, the prophetic use
of the *ríb* pattern, and the imagery typical of the prophetic
threats.

Prophet and Cult

H. Reventlow argues to a connection with a feast commemora-
ting Israel's covenant with Yahweh on the basis of a prophetic
'office'. The various literary forms used by the prophets are the
signs of this. These are the threats and promises, the indictments
and so forth, which characterize the prophetic books. They are
said to derive from the covenant feast and to be specifically the
work of an official in that cult whose duty was to proclaim
the traditional law, condemn disobedience and the like. Hence the
prophetic 'office'.[1] Strangely, though writing long after the discussion of the covenant form became prominent, he makes no

---

[1] On the preaching of the law see *Gebot und Predigt im Dekalog*, Gütersloh, 1962: on the prophetic 'office', *Wächter über Israel: Ezekiel und seine
Tradition*, *BZAW* 82, Berlin, 1962, and *Das Amt des Propheten bei Amos*,
Göttingen, 1962. Mowinckel, *Psalms in Israel's Worship*, vol. 1, 159–61,
had already pointed to a relation between the prophetic threats and
promises and the cultic affirmation of covenant.

allusion to it. As a matter of fact, his connection of the prophet with a covenant ritual could easily be turned into a connection with the covenant form.

W. Zimmerli does make this connection. His problem is the relationship of the prophets to law and the place of the law in Israelite religion. He sees the law as being derived from the covenant. He also considers the covenant to have had something of the treaty or covenant form, though he is properly cautious in his remarks about the way in which the historical relation between the Hittite treaty and Israel's covenant could have occurred. At any rate, the proclamation of the law was embedded in liturgical celebrations of the covenant which involved a reading of the law. Hence the prophets could and did preach on the basis of a law which they knew and which they expected their audience to know.[2]

Some of this argumentation seems too rigid. It is possible that the prophets knew and used forms of speech proper to or common in the cult without themselves having been officers in that cult. Just as they expected their hearers to be familiar with the law proclaimed to them in the liturgy, they could become familiar with the forms of that liturgy without having been officiants in it. Then it is or seems to be assumed that knowledge of the law could only be preserved in the cult. This is simply not the case. Family traditions and schools of wisdom were also at work, so that one cannot argue directly from a reference to law to a cultic connection. This is especially so when it is a question of basic prohibitions and admonitions. Finally, it sometimes seems as though the only possible source of a threat or a blessing or an apodictic law was the covenant or treaty form. This is not so. Human nature and human experience could supply them from many sources. In fact, curses especially but not exclusively (cf. our earlier discussion of apodictic law) are in evidence from many sources throughout ancient Near Eastern culture. Further, the reaction to Wellhausenian evolutionism with its view of the prophets as radical innovators, rebels, is healthy to a degree. It is certainly worthwhile to seek out the antecedents of the prophetic preaching. Still, the prophets were not at all confined to the old traditions. They had their own special experience, their own insights. They used old motifs to express them, but they

[2] *The Law and the Prophets*, Oxford, 1965, especially 52–7.

also could and did go far beyond these traditional forms and ideas.[3]

Some other studies of the prophecy-covenant relationship are perhaps closer to the texts. One which, like those we have been considering, uses what are thought to be aspects of the Israelite cult is W. Brueggemann's careful study of Amos 4:4-13. He finds that the passage affects the vocabulary of covenant and Holy War, e.g., 'prepare, fix' (*kûn*), 'meet' (*qr'*), possibly 'sacrifices' (*zᵉbaḥîm*), along with the familiar curses and blessings (here still presented as equally possible alternatives just as they are in the truest expressions of the covenant form.)[4] Further, there is reference to creation and theophany, both of which, following Mowinckel,[5] he takes to be elements in the Hebrew rites of covenant renewal. Two points should be noted here. First, Brueggemann finds the pericope uniting elements from the rites of the Holy War and the covenant, which indicates that the primitive separation of these two usages posited by Smend (above, nn. 14, 15) no longer obtained. Secondly, if a recalling of creation and a theophany were indeed part of official Hebrew covenant ceremonial, this seems to locate that covenant within

---

[3] This critique is developed in G. Fohrer, 'Remarks on the Modern Interpretation of the Prophets', *JBL* 80 (1961), 309-19, and R. Smend, *Bundesformel*, 23-5. R. E. Clements, *Prophecy and Covenant, Studies in Biblical Theology* 43, London, 1965, is an extensive and useful study in English of the ideas mentioned in the text and of much else. I would disagree with its blurring of the very real formal differences between the Davidic and Sinaitic covenants (cf. pp. 28, 50-2, 118: on the differences, L. Rost, 'Erwägungen zu Hos. 4; 13 ff.', *Bertholet Festschrift*, Tübingen, 1950, 460), the deduction of an expressed law from the mere fact of covenant (cf. pp. 105-6: promissory covenant, for example, does not necessarily have articulated stipulations or laws), and with the widely held idea that covenant and election are 'real' descriptions of the God–man relationship, while 'naturalistic' descriptions like father–son are simply 'imagery'. All discourse about God and his relation to man must be analogous or symbolic or in images because human language is inadequate to the reality: it is all, therefore, at once real (if it has any truth) and imagery. One regrets that a work so obviously carefully researched seems not to know *Biblica, Biblische Zeitschrift, CBQ, RB*, and the book series *Analecta Biblica*, all of which have carried materials pertinent to the theme of prophecy and covenant in recent years.

[4] 'Amos IV 4-13 and Israel's Covenant Worship', *VT* 15 (1965), 1-15.

[5] *Psalmenstudien*, Amsterdam, 1961, vol. 2.

ancient Near Eastern cultic traditions which are far removed from the treaty form of covenant.

The rîb *Pattern*

Studies of the *rîb* form, the prophetic lawsuit, have led to its being called the covenant lawsuit because it is said to reflect the covenant form.[6] In this form of suit the accused is summoned before the divine judge and called to account for his violations of his obligations. Particularly striking in this context is the recurrence of the appeal to heaven and earth and natural phenomena as witnesses. This appeal is characteristic in the treaties, and it appears in the Old Testament in Deut. 4 and 30 in speeches which may be modelled on the covenant form. It is rare in other ancient literature, though it does occur.[7] It is easy to see in this an appeal to witnesses who might have been invoked at the

---

[6] H. B. Huffmon, 'The Covenant Lawsuit and the Prophets', *JBL* 78 (1959), 286–95: J. Harvey, S.J., 'Le *'rîb*-Pattern'', réquisitoire prophétique sur la rupture de l'alliance', *Biblica* 43 (1962), 172–96: G. E. Wright, 'The Lawsuit of God: A Form-Critical Study of Deuteronomy 32', *Muilenburg Festschrift*, New York, 1962, 26–67.

[7] There is an invocation of natural phenomena in a Sumerian-Akkadian bilingual incantation text (E. Ebeling, *Archiv Orientální* 21 (1954), 380): F. M. Cross, 'Yahweh and the God of the Patriarchs', *Harvard Theological Review* 55 (1962), 246, n. 98, suggests that the reference to blessings from the heavens and from the deep in the Blessing of Jacob, Gen. 49:25–6, may also reflect the usage, and W. L. Moran, 'Some Remarks on the Song of Moses', *Biblica* 43 (1962), 317–20, discusses the same possibility in regard to Deut. 32:1. He also adduces two more extrabiblical examples; at Ugarit (cf. J. Nougayrol, *Palais royal d'Ugarit* IV, Paris, 1956, 137, 6 (= RS 18;06 + 17;365)) heaven and earth are invoked as witnesses to an international agreement (not strictly a treaty) between Ugarit and Amurru made under the aegis of the Hittite overlord, and in the Assyrian royal ceremonial (Frankena, *Takultu* 8, IX, 27 ff.) they are called on to bless the king. Thus in every instance there is question of oath, curse, or blessing. Surely this establishes a locus for the usage. The parallel between the OT texts and the extra-biblical material is denied by F. Nötscher, *Biblische Zeitschrift* 9 (1965), 207, on the plea that the 'orientalischen Vorliebe für . . . bildhafte Darstellung' by itself suffices to explain the usage, but the *Vorliebe* seems to have operated in this case exclusively in regard to oaths. To deny a parallel in such circumstances is to deny the possibility of any extrabiblical parallels. However, it must be admitted that, strictly speaking, here it shows a connection with oath-taking, not exclusively with the treaties, though oaths were important in them.

making of a covenant. Harvey's article goes even further and shows some similarities between these prophetic passages and the relics of some kind of formal prosecution of violators of treaties which are found in texts such as the Assyrian *Tukulti-Ninurta Epic* and in royal correspondence.[8]

Prophetic Threat and Treaty Curses

F. C. Fensham has catalogued a number of parallels between the curses which appear in the treaties and the threats called down upon the faithless people by the prophets.[9] This work has been carried farther and presented in greater detail in the work of Delbert Hillers in a very careful study which documents the parallels but is very conscious of the fact that there was a large general tradition of cursing in the ancient Near East and is careful about drawing conclusions as to historical connections.[10]

Thus there are signs that the prophets indicted Israel along lines suitable to the treaty tradition. This, of course, was because they had broken faith with Yahweh. Interestingly, before Ezekiel the prophets do not seem to have condemned the Hebrews for violating their inter-national agreements (2 Kgs. 18:25; Isa. 36:10). Thus the Assyrian claim to be attacking a faithless Judah with Yahweh's approval would not have been recognized at the time. Only in Ezekiel do we begin to find condemnation of the Israelites for breaking faith with other nations.[11]

Can we conclude that, though the earlier prophets may have known of treaties, they were not interested in them? This would, it seems, seriously weaken a claim that they knew the form and appealed to a treaty-type covenant when condemning Israel, but it might account for the notorious fact that *berît* (meaning both 'treaty' and 'covenant') is a rare word in their speeches. This fact has always caused commentators difficulty. It is one of the supports for Wellhausen's argument that the moral or legal covenant was a late development which followed from the prophets'

[8] See J. Harvey, op. cit., 182–8.

[9] 'Common Trends in the Curses of the Near Eastern Treaties and Kudurru-inscriptions Compared with the Maledictions of Amos and Isaiah', *ZAW* 75 (1963), 155–75.

[10] *Treaty-Curses and the Old Testament Prophets, Biblica et orientalia* 16, Rome, 1964.

[11] M. Tsevat, 'The Neo-Assyrian and Neo-Babylonian Oaths and the Prophet Ezekiel', *JBL* 78 (1959), 199–204.

insights. There have been frequent attempts to show that this
cannot be so because the prophets avoid the word only to avoid
the over-confidence which it induced. However, they are said to
have used the concept of covenant. This is seen in their demand
for absolute fidelity to Yahweh and his precepts and in their
warnings and promises. However, as has been said earlier, it is
difficult to prove that these concepts of fidelity and obedience
and the rest can only have flowed from the covenant concept or
the covenant form. Other reasons for fidelity are conceivable even
within the framework of Old Testament Yahwism.

The comparison with the *rîb* pattern is perhaps the most telling
argument for a connection with covenant, indeed, with covenant
in treaty form. Still, its strongest point is the invocation of
heaven and earth, and this could be a relic of oath forms common
to treaties and other situations (cf. the references in n. 7). One
might think of a ritual parallel with the treaties in some respects
but an independent development from the common oath forms.
Something like this has been suggested by Reventlow.

Or does the prophetic evidence show something else? The *rîb*
introduces the concept of keeping one's word into the description of Israel's relation to Yahweh. This would be part of the
process of making explicit what is implicit in any covenant relationship. It would be a step in the development from what I see
as the older, basically ritual forms of covenant (e.g., Sinai as
described in Exod. 19:24, 34) to the later covenant of the word
(Deuteronomy).[12] Such development may have been occasioned
by acquaintance with the treaties widely used by Assyria in
prophetic times, but it may also have come from familiarity with
solemn 'courtroom' procedures, oaths of fidelity elicited on
behalf of newly crowned kings, or the many other occasions for
oath-taking in ancient society.

[12] *Treaty and Covenant*, 172–7.

4

Human Covenants in Israel

So far we have been dealing with the various possible expressions of covenant relationship which were applied to the relation between Israel and Yahweh. If we are to understand the Israelite mentality regarding covenant, if we are to appreciate some of the resonance of the term and the concept in the Old Testament, we must not fail to look at some of the other kinds of covenant or covenant-making which were known and practised in ancient Israel. These were manifold, and they can hardly have failed to colour the meaning of covenant for the people, even when they were not directly applied to explain the special relation of the nation to its God.

The Multiplicity of Forms

The tremendous variety of forms available to create and to express a covenant can easily be seen by a glance at Pedersen's standard handbook, *Israel*. An exchange of gifts, the shaking of hands, the eating of something together, oath, and a host of other things, could be used to form covenantal relationships.[1] Apparently even ceremonies with oil could produce a covenant, an alliance between nations.[2] There is even another kind of covenant

[1] For a more recent study of some of the aspects of gift giving, sacrifice, covenant meal, oath and certain other kinds of covenant making attested in the Old Testament see D. J. McCarthy, S.J., 'Three Covenants in Genesis', *CBQ* 27 (1964), 179–89.

[2] D. J. McCarthy, S.J., 'Hosea XII 2; Covenant by Oil', *VT* 14 (1964), 215–21. K. Deller, 'šmn bll (Hosea 12;2). Additional Evidence', *Biblica* 46 (1965), 349–52, cites additional Akkadian texts which give evidence that oil could be involved in the making of pacts and covenants. He attempts to specify further how this worked. He suggests the use of

which is designated by the material apparently used in making it, the salt covenant. Generally, this has been thought to mean a covenant based on a communal meal (cf. the firm relationship established among bedouin by sharing 'bread and salt'), or, somewhat fancifully as it seems to me, on the symbolism of salt as a preservative. Now it is suggested that the salt refers to the curse element; certainly conquered rebels faced having their cities destroyed and strewed with salt.[3]

The odd name 'sons of Hamor' (*bhy ḥmwr* = 'sons of an ass') in Gen. 33:19 (= Josh. 24:32) has also been interpreted as relating to covenant, in fact, as meaning 'sons (i.e., partners) of covenant'. The basis for this is the fact that Shechem, the city involved in Gen. 34, worshipped a 'lord of covenant', plus the apparent use of the South Arabic cognate(?) *ḥmr* for 'pact'.[4] Finally, it has been suggested that we have a bit of covenant terminology in 1 Kgs. 12:16b: 'To your tents, Israel'. This may have meant the dissolution of the 'congregation' (*ʿēdāh, qāhāl*) which represented the people in making an agreement with the king.[5]

Gibeon and Tyre

Josh. 9, the treaty between the Israelites and the men of Gibeon, makes the latter the 'servants' (*ʿaebādîm*) of Israel and produces 'peace' (*šalôm*) between the parties.[6] There is also an oath and a covenant meal, while 2 Sam. 21:1–14, shows that conditional curses were involved, since Israel is punished for Saul's violation

lecanomancy in which the seer predicted the behaviour of the partners. This is based on translating CT 5, 5;45, *imitti awilim piam la kinam idabbub* as 'the man's right hand does not speak the truth', but this version has not been accepted. The suggestion remains a useful effort to fill a great need for specific knowledge of the details of ancient ritual. (See now K. R. Veenhof, *Bibliotheca orientalis* 23 (1966), 308–13, especially 312–13; oil was drunk or more probably smeared on the contracting party or parties, and its absorption symbolized taking on the conditional curse which was the oath (cf. Ps. 109:18).)

[3] F. C. Fensham, 'Salt as curse in the Old Testament and the Ancient Near East', *BA* 25 (1962), 48–50.

[4] F. Willesen, 'Die Eselsöhne von Sichem als Bundesgenossen', *VT* 14 (1964), 216–17.

[5] A. Malamat, 'Organs of Statecraft', *BA* 28 (1965), 39–40.

[6] F. C. Fensham, 'The treaty between Israel and the Gibeonites', *BA* 27 (1964), 96–100.

of the treaty. All this is indeed material standard in the covenant context, but it need not mean that the covenant *form* was used. Fensham himself depends on the Amarna letters to establish the covenant vocabulary on which his argument is partly based, and, while the Palestinian and other authors of the Amarna letters were certainly subordinate allies of Pharaoh, there is no evidence that their status depended upon treaties *in forma*. So also the covenant meal could be a source of union independent of the covenant form. However, we must admit a further link between the Gibeonite–Israel relationship and the treaty tradition. Another writer has pointed out that David's admission of guilt and his surrender of the sons of Saul to the Gibeonites to put aside the punishment visited on Israel because of its violation of a sworn treaty (2 Sam. 21:1–4) is closely parallel to the reaction of the Hittite King Mursilis II to a plague which he concluded to be a visitation on his people in punishment of his father's violation of a treaty with Egypt.[7]

The story of Solomon's dealings with Hiram of Tyre as pictured in 1 Kgs. 9:10–14 is also interesting. The Israelite king traded twenty cities for Phoenician lumber and gold. This is nothing very striking; such a use of real estate in their commercial dealings was commonplace among the kings of the time and place. Still, F. C. Fensham has been able to point out certain parallels with a treaty from the Syrian city of Alalakh between Abba-AN, king of Aleppo, and Yarimlim, a treaty which concerns an exchange of cities.[8] There are similarities in terminology: 'give' (*natan* in the Hebrew, *nadānu* in the Akkadian from Alalakh) is the operative verb describing the transaction, and the partner in each case is 'my brother' (Hebrew *'aḥî*, Akkadian *aḥiya*). Interestingly, Hiram must protest the decrepit state of the cities he received from the Israelite Solomon, while the gentile Abba-AN protests his reluctance to leave his 'brother' with a ruined city, let alone trade him one!

[7] A. Malamat, 'Doctrines of Causality in Hittite and Biblical Historiography', *VT* 5 (1955), 1–12.

[8] F. C. Fensham, 'The treaty between Solomon and Hiram and the Alalakh Tablets', *JBL* 79 (1960), 59–60. J. B. Priest has studied Amos 1:9 in the light of the Levantine–Aegean milieu ('Covenant of Brothers', *JBL* 84 (1965), 400–6) and concluded that the text refers to a treaty between Tyre and Israel according to the form common to the nations of the era.

Treaty Terminology and Maccabees

Finally we must note the work which has been done on covenant and treaty in the books of Maccabees.[9] According to Penna *synthēkē* is the normal word for 'treaty', and the Greek *diathēkē*, 'testament', is always used in a religious sense in these books except for 1 Macc. 1:11; 11:9 (pp. 179–80). The *synthēkē* is generally said to produce *eirēnē*, 'peace', *philia*, 'friendship', and *adelphotēs*, 'brotherhood', a vocabulary which reflects remarkably the ancient Semitic usage in which characteristically treaty or covenant produced (to use the basic Akkadian forms paralleled by cognates in Hebrew and translations in Hittite) *sulummu*, 'peace', *ṭabtu*, 'friendship' (see Moran, above, ch. 2, n. 10) and *aḫutu*, 'brotherhood'. On the other hand, Penna emphasizes that the Maccabean treaties '. . . omit any reference to rites or oaths . . . as well as clauses in favour of the Seleucids . . .' (technically, the overlords involved) (p. 155, n. 1). They, then, represent a radical departure from the older treaty form, even if they preserve some of its technical terminology.

[9] Briefly treated in J. Coppens, 'La doctrine biblique sur l'amour de Dieu et du prochain', *Ephemerides theologicae lovanienses* 40 (1964), 268, n. 59, and given an excellent treatment in detail in A. Penna, 'Διαθήκη e συνθήκη nei libri dei Maccabei', *Biblica* 46 (1965), 149–80.

5

Covenant and Kingship

There is a special problem with the Davidic covenant. There are those who believe that the monarchy was a dangerous institution, always in tension with true Yahwist covenant-thinking, which in fact corrupted Israel and made it necessary for a reform to return to the true covenant idea.[1] There are considerable difficulties in such a view.

Covenant and Royal Ideology

In fact, the scholars of the patternist persuasion who emphasize the primary place of the kingship in Hebrew religion would find it the exact reverse of the truth! One of them, G. Widengren, has tried to demonstrate the priority of the Davidic covenant.[2] He finds that texts like 1 Kgs. 8, 2 Kgs. 11 and 2 Kgs. 23, give a picture of the kings as custodians of the covenant law, empowered and obliged to preserve it and make it known. It was, therefore, the king who had the duty of proclaiming the law in the course of the covenant cult (pp. 2–9). Hence Deut. 17:14–20, does not denigrate the kingship, as is usually thought, but describes the king's rights and duties toward the fundamental law (p. 15). In fact, the Davidic covenant proclaimed in 2 Sam. 7 always included a juridical element, as several royal psalms

---

[1] So, with greater or lesser emphasis, J. Bright, *A History of Israel* (Philadelphia, n.d.), 203–8: A. Alt, 'Das Königtum in den Reichen Israel und Juda', *Kleine Schriften* II (Munich, 1959), 116–34 (= *VT* 1 (1951), 2–22 = *Essays on Old Testament History and Religion* (Oxford, 1966), 241–59.) Many more examples could be added.

[2] 'King and Covenant', *Journal of Semitic Studies* 2 (1957), 1–32: see also J. R. Porter, *Moses and Monarchy*, Oxford, 1963.

show (pp. 22–6). Even the roles of the heroes Joshua and Moses as teachers and custodians of the law are said really to be retro-jections of the king's office (pp. 15–20). The exaltation of the kingship in arguments of this sort is not widely accepted, and it is indeed probably exaggerated.[3] Still, the mere fact that a mass of plausible arguments of this kind can be accumulated is a warning against finding too negative an attitude toward kingship in the Old Testament.

The Restoration and Promissory Covenant

Apart from the problematic claim to pride of place for the king-ship in Hebrew religion, to so-called 'royal ideology', the central importance of the Davidic covenant is obviously a matter of con-cern in the Old Testament. Prophetic and historical books must and do deal with it, but the importance of the royal covenant pre-cisely as covenant is best illustrated by the problem of the restoration, the return from the exile which followed the Baby-lonion conquest of Jerusalem in 587 B.C. The restored community was confronted with the problem of its continuing existence even though it knew from the words of the prophets and from the actuation of the curses connected with the Deuteronomic covenant that the covenant had been broken. This had to mean the end of the covenant as such. This flowed from the very nature of the relationship described in the covenant form. It was con-ditioned on fidelity, and prophetic word and historical experience proved that the condition no longer obtained, so that the covenant must be at an end.[4] And yet the people of God remained. How could this be? How could there still be an Israel? To what did it owe its continuity as Yahweh's people? This was a real problem in O.T. theology.

This theological problem demanded an answer. This was pro-vided by an appeal to the promissory and absolute kind of covenant which had been given to David's line and to the Pat-riarchs.[5] That is to say, a covenant which was not formulated in

[3] See the important critical remarks of M. Noth, 'God, King, and Nation in the Old Testament', *The Laws in the Pentateuch and Other Essays*, Edinburgh, 1966, 145–78.

[4] Cf. W. Zimmerli, 'Das Gesetz im AT', *Gottes Offenbarung*, 270; *The Law and the Prophets*, 90–1.

[5] See Deut. 4:31 on the patriarchal covenant and the hopes of Haggai and Zechariah regarding the Davidids: discussion in N. Lohfink, S.J.,

terms of stipulations with attendant curses and blessings depending upon the keeping of the stipulations. No, this was a kind of covenant which was simply a promise of God and was valid despite anything Israel might do. Thus the form of the Davidic covenant was not only acceptable, it became the backbone of a theological structure which explains the continuity of Israel, a theological structure which is elaborated in later books of the Bible.

This is well illustrated in the books of Chronicles. Indeed, the Chronicler does not seem to consider the Mosaic covenant of prime importance. He avoids any mention of it and as far as possible any mention of Moses. His whole interest is concentrated on David and his covenant, the covenant which is connected with his beloved temple and its worship. Exodus and the Sinai covenants were in his opinion provisional, mere steps toward the full covenant which is that of David. He may even be said to have wished to rectify the false impression that the Sinai covenant was basic.[6] All this should not be understood as a contention that the post-exilic theology as seen in Chronicles considered Israel to be somehow confirmed in grace so that sin was no more a danger. This is definitely not the case. Ezra and Nehemiah display a lively sense of the people's obligation towards God and of the possibility of sin.[7] Just how this was to be integrated into the promissory form of covenant might still be considered a problem, but it is one little discussed and outside our present scope.

Further, it is to be noted that the post-exilic de-emphasis on the covenant mediated by Moses at Sinai is not without its forerunners. The priestly work (the P source of higher Pentateuchal criticism), surely representing a much older tradition than

'Die Wandlung des Bundesbegriffs im Buch Deuteronomium', *Rahner Festschrift*, Freiburg i. B., 1964, 430–1, 438–41.

[6] On this covenant theology of the Chronicler, see R. North, S.J., 'The Theology of the Chronicler', *JBL* 82 (1963), 376–80, A.-M. Brunet, 'La théologie du Chroniste; théocracie et messianisme', *Sacra Pagina*, 1, edited by J. Coppens, Gembloux-Paris, 1959, 391, and R. Schmid, *Das Bundesopfer*, 110–14, and J. Scharbert, *Heilsmittler im Alten Testament und im Alten Orient*, *Quaestiones disputatae* 23/4, Freiburg i. B., 1964, 145.

[7] D. N. Freedman, *Interpretation* 18 (1964), 430–1, discusses the problem.

Chronicles, seems to have dropped a formal covenant making at
Sinai. For it the important event there has become the fulfilment
of the covenant already made with Abraham through the divine
grant of the proper cultic law.[8] On the other hand, already in
Nathan's promise, that is, in the covenant with David, the grace
given David was extended to the whole people.[9] This idea was
developed in the exilic prophet called Deutero-Isaiah.[10]

Thus the promissory covenant, whether Davidic or patriarchal, has an important theological role. Since this is so, it is
remarkable that the resurgent interest in covenants and insights
into their nature has not produced more new study of the
covenant with the fathers.[11] The patriarchal covenant is still
spoken of as a 'structural accommodation to the Exodus story'
since the sentence 'I am Yahweh who led you out of Ur of the
Chaldees' echoes Exod. 20:2 and Deut. 5:6.[12] The idea that the
patriarchal covenant is a theological construct appears also in
H. Gese,[13] who also implies that all covenants were of one
promissory and absolute form. It is not clear in these instances
whether we are supposed to be dealing with entire constructs as
in the case of the critical school which takes the patriarchal
covenants to be simple extrapolations of the Davidic covenant,[14]
or have to do with reconstructions of real earlier covenants in
later theological terms. There is good reason to hold a basis in
fact. Since Alt's 'The God of the Fathers' we have known that the
irrevocable promise by the 'god of the fathers' to the patriarchs
was something characteristic of the religion of nomads on the way

[8] See W. Zimmerli, 'Sinaibund und Abrahambund', *Gottes Offenbarung*, 212–13.

[9] D. J. McCarthy, S.J., 'II Samuel 7 and the Structure of the Deuteronomic History', *JBL* 84 (1965), 132.

[10] So O. Eissfeldt, 'The Promises of Grace to David in Isaiah 55:1–5',
Muilenburg Festschrift, 196–207.

[11] But see H. Cazelles, 'Connexions et structure de Gen. XV', *RB* 69
(1962), 321–49.

[12] W. Zimmerli, 'Promise and Fulfilment', *Essays in Old Testament
Hermeneutics* (ed. C. Westermann and J. L. Mays), Richmond, Va.,
1964, 91. See also D. N. Freedman, *Interpretation* 18 (1964), 427.

[13] 'The Idea of History in the Ancient Near East and the Old Testament', *Journal for Theology and Church* 1, New York, 1965 (German
original, 1958).

[14] So A. Caquot, 'L'Alliance avec Abram (Genèse 15)', *Semitica* 12
(1962), 51–66.

to sedentarization.[15] Hence the fact of such a promise is plausible. Further, since such a promise was *ipso facto* a covenant of one sort, it is entirely reasonable to hold some form of actual covenant with the patriarchs, even though this conclusion seems not to have been drawn from Alt's work very often, if at all. Also, from the theological point of view von Rad has emphasized that the promissory covenant with Abraham (Gen. 12:1–3) cannot be thought of as a pale and otiose reflection of either Sinai or Nathan's promise.[16]

Covenant with David and the Sinai Covenant

More attention has been given to the Davidic covenant, and some effort has been made to integrate it with the Mosaic. This has been attempted, for example, by C. Schedl in an article on the function of prophets in the history of salvation.[17] He starts with the assumption that the Sinai covenant was a vassal treaty in form. This is what is supposed to have introduced the concept of conditioned blessing and curse into Israel's history. If Israel keeps the covenant it will be blessed, if not cursed. And it is precisely the function of the prophets to warn Israel when it is in danger of breaking the covenant, to condemn it when it has broken the covenant, and to encourage it to keep the covenant. He then proceeds to integrate the kingship into the whole by means of prophecy. The messianic prophecies of Isaiah are

[15] *Essays on Old Testament History and Religion*, 1–100 (German originally published in 1929). See also J. P. Hyatt, 'Yahweh as the God of My Father', *Vetus Testamentum* 5 (1955), 130–6, and especially F. M. Cross 'Yahweh and the God of the Patriarchs', *Harvard Theological Review* 55 (1962), 225–59.

[16] *Genesis, OT Library*, London, 1961, 154–6.

[17] 'Die heilsgeschichtliche Funktion der Propheten', *Bibel und Kirche* 19 (1964), 9–12. S. Mowinckel, *He That Cometh*, New York/Nashville, 1954, 99, 165–6, bases the integration rather on his concept of the king as centre of the covenant cult in Israel, while A. H. J. Gunneweg, 'Sinaibund und Davidsbund', *Vetus Testamentum* 10 (1960), 338–40, believes that the Davidic theology developed Israelite religion by showing through the royal ideology and its cultic expression that Yahweh is lord of fertility as well as history, and this depended on the dynasty's success in making itself guardian of the amphictyonic religion by moving the ark to Sion. Thus it integrated the Sinaitic amphictyony with kingship even though *in se* the *nichtstaatliche* amphictyony was incompatible with the royal state.

paradigmatic, and they are essentially promises of salvation; therefore, they are connected with the covenant because the origin of the promise of salvation was the blessing of the covenant. So, when Isaiah promises a splendid successor to David, he is making the Davidic line the vehicle by which the covenant blessing will be carried on. There is no discussion of the Davidic covenant as such, but this covenant surely was by itself the origin of blessings and prophecies of blessing.

Another very interesting attempt to integrate the Davidic covenant into the whole of the O.T., and specifically the Sinai covenant conceived of as a vassal treaty, is that of Roland de Vaux.[18] He finds that the anointed Davidic king is set by Yahweh over his people; so too was the vassal given his kingship by the sovereign. David was the servant of Yahweh; so too the vassal must serve his overlord. The Davidic king was guaranteed divine protection and this guarantee, the community between sovereign and overlord, continued on to the people; so also the vassal enjoyed the protection of the overlord, and the people are sometimes included in the treaty. This protection depended upon the Davidic king's fidelity; so too the vassal treaties' continuation depended upon the vassal's fidelity. The vassal treaty contained stipulations which were written down in a carefully preserved document; so according to 2 Kgs. 11:12, the Davidic king received the testimonies (*'ēdut*), which would appear to be a list of the laws to which he must be faithful. De Vaux concludes that the Davidic king was thus the vassal of Yahweh in virtue of a covenant in strict vassal-treaty form.

This would be proven only if this relationship alone could result in the factors elaborated by de Vaux. But this is simply not so: men were chosen by Yahweh, men were spoken of as his servants, without any question of a special vassal covenant between Yahweh and the men in question. The Davidic covenant is indeed extended through David to the people in the famous promise of Nathan in 2 Sam. 7, but it is rare that the people are included explicitly in the vassal treaties. This does occur, for instance in the treaty of Suppiluliumas with Huqqanas and the people of Hayasa, and in the Aramaic treaty from Sefire. In the treaties with the men of Ismirik and of Kaska the peoples them-

---

[18] 'Le roi d'Israël, vassal de Yahvé', *Tisserant Festschrift, Studi e testi* 231, Vatican City, 1964, 119–33.

selves, without mention of king or leader, are partners of the
Hittite king. These instances are exceptions dictated by circumstances (an almost barbarian tribe with its leader, a coalition, and
another tribe respectively are involved in these treaties),[19] not
by the treaty form as such. Thus the most we can claim is that
this feature of the Davidids' position, the explicit extension of
their dynastic covenant to their people, is compatible with the
treaty form, but it need not in any way have been dictated by it.
Further, the permanence of the Davidic covenant as described in
the basic statement of it is not dependent upon the fidelity of the
Davidids; on the contrary, the promise of Nathan says explicitly
that even though the king is faithless, his position will be
assured. This is the direct contrary of the case in the formal
treaty. It is true that in Ps. 132 there is an apparent conditioned
statement of the Davidic covenant: if the Davidids are faithful,
they will reign for ever over Israel. However, even here we have
but this one element of the covenant form, and it is connected
with the Zion cult. This is a covenant which is granted David and
his line in view of the cult that they have instituted in Jerusalem.[20]
This brings us into the realm of the theology of Zion with its
basic tenet of the indefectibility of the Jerusalem worship. Since
Ps. 132 makes the connection of this worship with the Davidids
a necessity, the condition imposed on the permanence of the
dynasty is not very serious. In fact, it is unreal. If Zion must
endure, so must the dynasty linked with it.

On the other hand, de Vaux is very convincing when he goes on
to show that anointing was known among the Hittites and
especially among the Egyptians, where vassals were bound to
Pharaoh himself and at the same time received their kingship by
accepting his anointing. Thus the anointing of the king signifies
his vassalship, his special union with the divine sovereign of
Egypt giving him a kind of untouchable holiness himself. Here is
a sign, a rite constituting a vassal kingship with all the features

[19] For references to the publications and discussion of these and other
treaty texts see the Bibliography and Indices in D. J. McCarthy, S.J.,
Treaty and Covenant. (See now also E. von Schuler, *Die Kaškäer*, Berlin,
1965, for texts and studies of the Hittite treaties with the Kaska.)
[20] See H. Gese, 'Der Davidsbund und die Zionserwählung', *Zeitschrift
für Theologie und Kirche* 61 (1964), 10–16. G. von Rad, *Old Testament
Theology*, Edinburgh, 1965, 155–75, studies the Davidic (Messianic)
and Jerusalemite Zion traditions and their linking in Isaiah.

characteristic of the position of Yahweh's anointed king. Indeed, even the 'testimonies' given the king at his coronation, the one factor not explained by the analogy with the Egyptian anointing, has been related to Egyptian royal ceremonial.[21]

[21] See G. von Rad, 'The Royal Ritual in Judah', *The Problem of the Hexateuch*, 222–31; G. Fohrer, 'Der Vertrag zwischen König und Volk in Israel', *ZAW* 71 (1959), 3, proposes the thesis that the 'testimonies' were actually laws defining and limiting the king's power in relation to the people (cf. 1 Sam. 10:25), and not his special relation to God. On the anointing itself see now A. Malamat, *The Biblical Archaeologist* 28 (1965), 65, and especially E. Kutsch, *Salbung als Rechtsakt im AT und im Alten Orient*, *BZAW* 87, Berlin, 1963, 55–63, 71–2: the anointing expresses the divine aspect of the king's position, God's approval of his authority.

6

Covenant and Theology

Up to this point we have been largely concerned with the literary and historical aspects of covenant. There have also been recent discussions of the theological implications of covenant and specifically of the covenant form. Even the historical reconstruction which we have already seen, namely, the view that there was a sort of pure Mosaism expressed in a covenant in the treaty form, a falling away from this caused largely by the institution of the monarchy, and a call for a return to pure Mosaism in the prophets which was partly answered by the Deuteronomic reform under Josiah, certainly has its theological implication.

Law and Gospel

Then there is the classic problem of covenant as law opposed to the Gospel of grace. The discovery that the law was not an antecedent means of meriting a special relationship to God, but rather the very definition and stuff of that relationship already constituted by the grace of election and covenant, has changed the whole case. For one thing, one does not earn a closeness to God by means of the law. Then, if law is essentially a part of covenant, God, who freely gives the covenant, can and does implicitly promise the grace needed to live by that law. The law does not earn God's grace. It is rather a result of grace and the definition of one's life as an actual relationship to God.[1]

However, the problem is complicated by the varieties of form

[1] See M. G. Kline, 'Law and Covenant', *Westminster Theological Journal* 27 (1964), 1–20: H. Wildberger, *Jahwes Eigentumsvolk*, 113–17: R. Smend, *Bundesformel*, 29–31, and especially M. Noth, 'The Laws in the Pentateuch', *Laws*, 1–60.

in which the covenants between Yahweh and his people are
expressed. There is, after all, the promissory covenant in which
Yahweh commits himself to Israel apparently without conditions. D. N. Freedman has devoted a study to this problem of
divergent covenantal forms.[2] He finds that the actual presentation
of the covenant with the Patriarchs has undergone some influence
from the different form of the Sinai covenant. Still, the patriarchal covenant is basically one of promise. God commits himself
to the family of Abraham. This sort of promissory covenant is
presented in the Old Testament as following upon signal acts of
obedience, whether the covenant in question be that with the
Patriarchs or with David, but it cannot be said to be precisely
earned. In any event, the continuation of such a covenant is not
dependent upon the obedience of the human party; it remains
pure grace on God's part. Conversely the covenant in treaty form
is conditional. It could be broken, and when it was it needed to
be renewed. In fact, it needed periodic renewal in any case, just as
with ordinary treaties between civil states. Finally, Freedman
finds that the conditional covenant, that is, for him, the Sinai
covenant, is presented as being based on the promise to the
Patriarchs. Thus grace comes first; it is a condition for the law
rather than a consequence earned through the law.

To a considerable extent this parallels the results of a very
different study by U. Devescovi.[3] Written in Italian and published in Macao, this is not a book which has received or will
receive much attention. Yet it makes some important points.
Perhaps most important of all is the general principle laid down
at the beginning: Whatever may be the pre-history of our biblical text, whatever its written sources or the oral traditions on
which it drew, what counts for the theologian is the final text
given to us in its present order and organization. Of course, this
does not mean that we should ignore the pre-history of a text.
On the contrary, the best, indeed the only way to understand a
biblical text which is normally the result of a long and complex
history of formation is to study its growth. The study of the
history of the forms used in the Bible and of the editorial modi-
fications necessitated by their combination into larger wholes
(*Redaktionsgeschichte*) yields the most revealing indications of the

[2] *Interpretation* 18 (1964), 427.
[3] *L'alleanza nell' Esateuco*, Macao, 1957.

intention of the whole. We cannot dispense with the historical growth of the text, but we should not become so intrigued by the search for antecedents that we forget the final text itself.[4]

As a theologian, then, Devescovi properly treats the sequence of covenants as they stand in the Bible. On this basis he finds three essentials in the first special covenant, that with Abraham, the promises of freedom, of a special relation to God, and of possession of Canaan. These are fulfilled in the exodus, the Sinai covenant, and the progress towards and conquest of Canaan as told in the first books of the Bible. Thus law and felicity are the fulfilment of grace, not vice versa.[5]

A further theological topic upon which the covenant concept has been asked to cast light is the problem of human freedom and responsibility. God does not force himself and his covenant on the people. Rather he presents them with a choice and persuades them to accept freely a special relation to himself. The point is developed by J. Héléwa.[6] He finds the classic proposition placing the choice before Israel of a covenant with Yahweh or another god in Exod. 19:3–8, the conclusion of the chosen covenant in Exod. 24:3–8, and an example of renewal in Josh. 24. However, not only the first proposition but all these texts and the others concerned with covenant are shot through with persuasion; the people are asked, never compelled, to enter into the relationship.

Héléwa's point is important and in general well made. However, he actually weakens his case by insisting unnecessarily on

---

[4] More and more it is being realized that the Bible is to be treated as a whole and not interpreted according to separate units: cf. N. Lohfink, S.J., 'Uber die Irrtumslosigkeit und die Einheit der Schrift', *Stimmen der Zeit* 174 (1964), 161–81 (=*Das Siegeslied am Schilfmeer*,[2] Frankfurt, 1966, 44–80: English summary in *Theology Digest* 13 (1965), 185–92).

[5] The law-gospel problem is often thought to be specifically Protestant, but the relation of law and grace is a general Christian question, and Catholic scholars have addressed it in the Old Testament, and like Devescovi they have reached answers similar to those referred to in the text: cf. M. O'Connell, 'The Concept of Commandment in the Old Testament', *Theological Studies* 21 (1960), 351–403: P. van Imschoot, *Théologie de l'Ancien Testament, Bibliothèque de théologie III: Théologie biblique* 2, Tournai, 1954, 244–55: N. Lohfink, S.J., 'Gesetz und Gnade', *Das Siegeslied am Schilfmeer*,[2] Frankfurt, 1966, 151–73.

[6] Jean Héléwa de la Croix, O.D.C., 'Alliance Mosaïque et liberté d'Israël', *Ephemerides carmeliticae* 16 (1965), 3–40; see also P. Buis et J. Leclercq, *Le deutéronome*, 21.

finding the covenant form in all the texts which concern him: *Qui nimis probat*—! This is not to deny or affirm that the form is in fact there; in either case it is not really relevant. The persuasion as opposed to coercion is in the texts as they stand, whatever their form. Always we have a speaker trying to convince rather than a powerful ruler forcing assent. It may even be that preaching, persuasion devoted to religious purposes, as developed in the Deuteronomic school, had some relation to the covenant form. However, this, in so far as it is related to a concern for the freedom of the auditors, is a special development for which the historical role of the treaty did not prepare except perhaps formally in the narrow sense, as in 'formality'. The Hittite king often seems to persuade his vassal, as, in a way, does the Assyrian when he confronts the vassal with the horrid fate of the rebel. However, treaties were really the result of force, not persuasion, a fact that often enough shows through in the texts. In any event, it is not possible nor particularly desirable to reduce all concern for the freedom of the person to the concept behind the treaty form of covenant. What matters is the fact that the texts themselves, whatever their form, aim to persuade and not to coerce assent.

Openness of the Old Testament Covenant

A final point of theological interest does rest upon the formulation of the covenant in terms of threats and blessings. This shows that Israel did not live simply in fear and danger because of the law. It did indeed respect Yahweh, but reasonably and religiously. Neither was it blithely and unthinkingly sure of grace. The threats and the blessings kept before it the possibilities of sin and failure or grace and success. Hence the open-ended character of Old Testament religion which is emphasized in the prophets, who dwell now upon judgement, now upon hope. Thus the covenant in what may seem its most formal, legalist expression, in the treaty form, contributes to the openness of the Old Testament to further development in the New.[7]

[7] W. Zimmerli, *The Law and the Prophets*, 59–60, 93–96.

7

Conclusions

Perhaps we can now sum up the present state of the question in regard to Old Testament Covenant. Surely the treaty form was known in Israel, and it seems to have been used as an analogy to describe the relation between the nation and Yahweh. Many would say that this form and concept of covenant appear in the basic covenant described in the events at Sinai in Exod. 19–24, 34, and that they have left perhaps their clearest traces in the Decalogue. Others—and I would agree—deny this. The Sinai texts do not show the covenant form, and the origins of apodictic law and so of the Decalogue are to be sought elsewhere than in the treaties.

The appearance of the *rîb* pattern, the covenant law-suit, in some prophetic texts, may indicate that they knew something like the covenant form and that they applied it to the relationship between Yahweh and Israel. However this may be, it is clear enough that the prophets arraigned Israel for something like the breaking of an oath.

It seems quite certain that the form is used in Deuteronomy. It seems to appear also in some other passages, mostly speeches, connected in one way or another with the Deuteronomistic school. It has been suggested that the covenant form may have been a northern institution. Evidence is adduced to connect it with Shechem and perhaps Gilgal. The different form of covenant which appears in the Sinai texts may have been the opposite number to the northern institution among the tribes of the south. Much work remains to be done in tracing the history and milieu of the form within the Hebrew people.

There can be no doubt that covenant was connected with cult. The importance of sacrifice and the theophany as exemplified in the Sinai narratives, for instance, show this. Moreover, it is striking that the apparent sequence of certain ceremonies reflects in large part the sequence of the elements in the treaty documents. This raises the vexed question of the covenant feast. There was surely a ceremony which instituted covenant and repaired or renewed it when it was broken or when some major change in the circumstances of the people made them feel the need for renewal. The question of a regularly recurring covenant feast is another matter.

The relationship between the prophets and covenant needs further study. Work on the curses and condemnations of the prophets shows that they use imagery analogous to that of the covenant curses. However, these curses were part of the common Near Eastern patrimony. They occur in other kinds of documents such as the boundary stones, the law codes, and the building inscriptions of the area. Do they show a relation between prophetic speech and the covenant form? Or does the *rib* pattern? It is impossible to give an apodictic answer. And still the troubling question remains: Why do the prophets avoid the word 'covenant'?[1]

Finally, the relationship between the Davidic and the Mosaic covenants remains to be clarified. Was there a serious tension, even an opposition, or, as some extreme proponents of this idea hold, a basic incompatibility between them? The kingship is a basic element in Old Testament theology and of supreme importance because of its role in developing messianic ideas. We have seen that the attempt to make the Davidic covenant formally identical with the Mosaic on the basis of a covenant form common to the two has failed. The Davidids did have a special relation to Yahweh, and this is tied up with their role as patrons of the Temple worship. Moreover, this relationship was in the form of a promissory, an absolute covenant. The family of David will be favoured and through them the people will receive grace in spite of their failures. This is not in form or content a covenant of the treaty type. How did Israel integrate this into the Mosaic covenant in its various expressions?

[1] It would be interesting to know whether there is a definite pattern of occurrence of the *rib* pattern and the treaty-like curses among the prophets according to whether they had northern or southern affinities, but we are warned that in regard to the curses 'statistical measurement is not possible' (Hillers, *Treaty-Curses*, 77).

8

Postscript

As the preface said, this section attempts to bring the book up to date. It notes important materials overlooked in the original edition as well as those published since it appeared. Considerations of space must keep it short. Failure to discuss a work is not a value judgment on it. Often studies of details, for instance, have the most enduring value, but in the nature of the case they cannot always be touched here. Brevity also will call for a terseness of presentation. This can often fail to do complete justice to a subject, but it is inevitable in any survey. I hope this will be understood and forgiven.

Philology and berît

O. Loretz develops the suggested connection with (not necessarily the derivation from) Akkadian *bi/ertu*, 'fetter', via the middle-Assyrian form *berittu*, where the double consonant suggests a compensation for a long vowel and so a perfect correspondence with *berît*.[1] Semantic parallels, Ugaritic *mṣmt*, 'contract', (root *ṣmd*, 'tie') and Akkadian *riksu*, 'contract, treaty' (root *rakāsu*, 'bind') bear this out.

E. Kutsch has studied the use of *berît* in older biblical texts.[2] He finds three basic meanings: (1) obligation taken on oneself without expectation of a return; (2) obligation laid on another without taking one upon oneself; (3) mutually assumed obligations. Only the first two meanings are pertinent to Israel's covenant with God (Yahweh's binding promise to Abraham, and

[1] 'בדיח—"Band, Bund" ', *VT* 16 (1966), 239–41.

[2] 'Der Begriff *berît* in vordeuteronomischer Zeit', *Rost Festschrift*, 133–43: 'Gesetz und Gnade. Probleme des alttestamentlichen Bundesbegriff', *ZAW* 79 (1967), 18–35.

in Hos. 8:1 the parallel of *bᵉrît* with torah binding Israel are respective examples). *bᵉrît* never means a relationship, an alliance, or covenant, but always obligation! Some of Kutsch's examples are unconvincing, e.g. his failure to note the mutual oath in Gen. 26:31, leading to a misunderstanding of 26:28, and his interpretation of Isa. 28:15 as an obligation making Death bypass Jerusalem. Such instances raise doubts about his novel claim that *bᵉrît* originally *always* meant obligation; it has long been known that it sometimes did. His theological conclusion that *bᵉrît*, meaning at once promise from God and obligation on man, reconciles grace and law has been reached by means of other views of *bᵉrît* or covenant, as we have seen.

An important element in Kutsch's argument is the close connection between *bᵉrît* and *nšbʿ*, 'swear'. This is taken up in N. Lohfink's study of Gen. 15.[3] It claims that in the oldest layers of J *bᵉrît* means or implies an oath. The argument which turns on taking Gen. 24:7 (with explicit mention of *nšbʿ*) as a reference to Gen. 15:18 (lacking *nšbʿ*) is weak. In Gen. 24:7 *nšbʿ* is textually uncertain, and the citation (imperfect first person singular of *ntn*) seems to look to Gen. 12:7 (identical form), not 15:18 (perfect). What Gen. 24:7 does show is that God's word (*dibbēr*) or speech (*'āmar*) is as good as an oath. It does not need the technical *nšbʿ* to strengthen it. The argument from Gen. 15:9–11: 17, is better, for it connects *bᵉrît* with what seems to be an acted-out self-cursing, a symbolic oath.

Not so long ago I would have accepted this without question, but now I am less certain. H. Cazelles has pointed out that the verb for dividing the animals is the piel of *šlš*. It must mean 'cut three times' (and so into four parts) or 'cut into three parts'.[4]

---

[3] *Die Landesverheissung als Eid*, Stuttgarter-Bibelstudien 28, Stuttgart, 1967. M. G. Kline, 'Abram's Amen', *Westminster Theological Journal* 31 (1968), 2–3, applies the concept of the delocative (a stock phrase or word turned into a verb (as in American English the noun 'author' becomes the verb 'to author', i.e. act as an author, write)) to Abraham's response in 15:6 (*h'myn*, usually translated 'he believed') and finds the sense 'he said "Amen" to, he agreed', that is, he responded with the ritual agreement of the inferior to an offer of covenant. Such an interpretation would surely affirm that an oath is involved, though not an oath by Yahweh as Lohfink contends. Kline cites as a parallel Num. 20:21, where he translates *h'myn 't*; 'Sihon did not declare "Amen" with Israel', i.e., rejected an offer to enter into a treaty or covenant.

[4] 'Connexions et Structure de Gen. XV', *RB* 69 (1962), 321–49.

Perhaps the latter is more likely, since two things pass together between the divided pieces in v. 17, indicating two paths and three parts. In any case, the rite is not identical with that in Jer. 34:18, to which it is usually referred. Now, we have considerable evidence of animal rites in covenant-making of the second millennium (to which Lohfink would seem to assign the substance of what is described in Gen. 15:9-11, 17)—cf. my *Treaty and Covenant*, 52-4—but explicit statement of the meaning, acted-out curse, comes much later in the Assyrian treaty with Mati-ilu of Arpad (eighth century B.C.) and Jeremiah. One wonders whether we do not face another case of a rite receiving an explanation long after its beginning, one perhaps different from the original meaning (if this were ever explicated).

Apart from these detailed studies, L. Köhler's excellent review of the history of the covenant idea in Israel deserves mention.[5] He emphasizes the importance of a peasant culture and its feeling for permanence and security as a background for the development of the reassuring covenant idea. This view of the setting of covenant should get more attention.

Finally, there is the problem of the Septuagint's use of *diathēkē* for *berît*, 'testament' and not 'alliance'. J. Swetnam has a suggestion worth following up. Egyptian papyri seem to indicate that *diathēkē* was used of a fictive 'willing' of a slave to a god or temple, a form of manumission.[6] The concept of a link with the divine bringing with it freedom has obviously rich theological dimensions.

Covenant as Idea and Institution

Most significant here is the questioning of the Sellin-Noth hypothesis of a union of groups, some related, some not, into a league at Shechem which is called, by analogy with Greek institutions, an amphictyony. The constitution which cemented this league together was supposed to be a common covenant with Yahweh which is reflected in Josh. 24.[7] Many think that this covenant is best conceived of as an adaptation of the ancient vassal treaty.

[5] *Old Testament Theology*, London, 1967, 65-75.

[6] '*Diathēkē* in the Septuagint Account of Sinai: A Suggestion', *Biblica* 47 (1966), 438-44. Considerable documentation for the secular use of *diathēkē* in the sense indicated is included.

[7] A good review of the importance of the covenant idea in this union is now available in English: cf. M. Noth, 'The Laws in the Pentateuch', *The Laws . . . and Other Studies*, 1-107.

The tribes and their members were joined together as vassals of the one sovereign god, and they accepted as their own a common pre-history and a set of basic duties.[8] G. Schmitt thinks that such an organization based on the treaty form could not have arisen during Israel's nomadic life in the south since the treaty was characteristic of settled states more to the north, with contacts, direct or indirect, with Hatti. Yet (according to Schmitt) the events at Sinai experienced in the south by nomads come to be described in treaty form. This is best explained by Israel's having interpreted its Sinai experience in terms of the vassal treaty which it came to know in connection with the Shechemite cult of Baal-berith.[9]

There are convincing arguments against this view. R. E. Clements notes that Josh. 24, reflecting an Israelite covenant ceremony at Shechem, does not really show the treaty form. It is, then, unlikely that Israel came to know and use this form at Shechem in connection with the Baal-berith cult.[10] In fact, the

[8] Cf. D. Hillers, *Covenant: The History of a Biblical Idea*, 68–70: J. Gray, *I and II Kings*, index s.v. 'covenant'.

[9] G. Schmitt, *Der Landtag zu Sichem*, 87–8; the idea had been advanced before, of course: e.g., J. Pedersen, *Israel* III–IV, 508. J. Gray, *Joshua, Judges and Ruth, The Century Bible*,² London and Edinburgh, 1967, 32–7, 191–200, also believes that Josh. 24 'is an account of an ancient transaction', that is, of covenant renewal inserted into the Book of Joshua either to give this important act of the hero greater emphasis or to associate the Law (tied to covenant) and the Conquest. The covenantal character of the transaction is clear from the parallel with the ancient treaty (which, he correctly notes, was a form common to ancient international law and in use well into the first millennium B.C., not something peculiar to the Hittites before 1200: hence his arguments for the antiquity of the underlying scheme are not based on the tricky formal parallels). He also accepts the affinity with Exod. 23:20–33 pointed to by Schmitt as an argument for the covenantal character of the text. *Contra* the Sellin-Noth hypothesis of a ceremony at Shechem in which the tribal league (amphictyony) was brought into being, Gray holds that Israel was already a people united by covenant. The Shechem ceremony will have been needed as a renewal stressing the exclusive relation of the covenanted community to Yahweh, an action especially needed during the first contact with polytheistic (and culturally superior) Canaan. Thus the passage reflects an historical occasion, and the ancient liturgy of covenant renewal is clearly reflected in it. However, in its present shape Josh. 24 is a rather free literary composition using other material besides the covenant liturgy to form an appendix to Josh. 23 and a more pointed introduction to the story of the judges.

[10] 'Baal-Berith of Shechem', *JSS* 13 (1968), 21–32.

kind of covenant native to Shechem was a 'ruler' covenant, a league between an oligarchy (or king) and a god by virtue of which they ruled. The Abimelech episode in Judg. 9 hints at this and also shows its incompatibility with Israelite ethos.

Still, it remains a commonplace to speak of pre-monarchical Israel as an amphictyony. One reason is the retention of the number of twelve tribes. The names of the member groups change, but the total is always twelve (or perhaps very early six, for six or a multiple of it was needed so that each member group could serve the common shrine for a month or two during the lunar year.) However, it should be noted that what remains the most complete study of the Greco-Latin amphictyonies[11] indicates that though the best known, the Delphic league, insisted on twelve and twelve only members, others did not. Further, after it has been shown that an amphictyony(?) nearer Israel and connected with the Aegean world (or at least the Sea-Peoples) probably did not have six members (see above, ch. 1, n. 16), Hanna Kassis has cast doubt on Gath's being a member of the Philistine league.[12] Its membership may be reduced to four! This might connect it with other tetrapolis groupings in Canaan, Gibeon (cf. Josh. 9:17) and Hebron (cf. its old name, Kiriath Arba, 'four cities').[13] Four goes into twelve, so that a connection with the lunar year remains possible, but the crucial multiple of six is still lost. It is even worse when one speaks of a ten-member amphictyony.[14]

One suspects that leagues were common, but it is hard to show that they are in any sense amphictyonies. In 1962 Orlinsky had already pointed out that 'amphictony' was hardly an appropriate name for pre-monarchical Israel.[15] The tribes were too inde-

[11] Cauer, 'Amphictyonia', Pauly-Wissowa, *Enzyclopädie der Altertumswissenschaft*, vol. 1 (1898!). We badly need a modern study of the Greco-Latin phenomenon.

[12] 'Gath and the Structure of the "Philistine" Society', *JBL* 84 (1965), 258–71.

[13] J. Blenkinsopp, 'Are There Traces of the Gibeonite Covenant in Deuteronomy?' *CBQ* 28 (1966), 207–19.

[14] Cf. S. Mowinckel, *Zur Frage nach dokumentarischen Quellen in Joshua*, Oslo, 1946, 13–19.

[15] 'The Tribal System of Israel . . . in the Period of the Judges', *Oriens antiquus* 1 (1962), 11–20: see now the forceful arguments of G. Fohrer, 'AT—"Amphiktyonie" und "Bund"', *TLZ* 91 (1966), 802–16, 893–904.

pendent, there is no evidence for any kind of central administration, and especially no single cult centre. Smend, seconded by S. Hermann,[16] has shown that the Ark was not a centre of worship which might make up for the lack of a central shrine, nor was it the palladium for the amphictyonic Holy War, as posited by G. von Rad.[17]

The study of ancient Syro-Palestinian society has created more problems for the amphictyonic hypothesis. M. Liverani[18] points out that the vassal-sovereign concept was very much alive in Palestine in the second half of the second millennium B.C. However, the leagues formed under its aegis shifted constantly. Thus it did not provide for the kind of stability posited by the amphictyonic idea. Worse, in the latter part of the era Egyptian control introduced new ideas which undermined the concept and made for even greater instability in theory as well as practice.

In his very important *Cities and Nations of Ancient Syria*,[19] G. Buccellati studies the socio-political structures of the whole of Syria and Palestine. On this basis he emphatically rejects the amphictyony analogy. (1) The very name, 'dwellers round', falsely suggests settled conditions around a fixed shrine, but (2) in the era of the judges Israel's traditions still centred around the very different conditions of a nomadic heritage, and (3) there was no fixed shrine. Further, (4) amphictyony implies a central administration which pre-monarchic Israel lacked, while (5) Israel had a comprehensive social order common to all its members and the true amphictyonies typically did not. Hence, while the study of the omnipresent phenomenon of Syrian leagues is fruitful for the understanding of Israel's condition,[20] the name 'amphictyony' is misleading and should be abandoned.

This makes sense. It is hard to maintain any specific points of similarity between the Israelite league and an amphictyony.

[16] 'Neuere Arbeiten zur Geschichte Israels', *TLZ* 89 (1964), 816–19.

[17] *Studies in Deuteronomy*, c. IV. Followed to some extent by J. A. Soggin, 'Zwei umstrittene Stellen aus dem Überlieferungskreis um Shechem', *ZAW* 73 (1961), 80.

[18] 'Contrasti e confluenze di concezioni politiche nell'età di el-Amarna', *Revue d'assyriologie* 61 (1967), 1–18.   [19] *Studi semitici* 26, Rome, 1967.

[20] For example, A. Malamat, 'Aspects of the Foreign Policies of David and Solomon', *JNES* 22 (1963), and B. Mazar, 'The Aramaean Empire and its Relations with Israel', *BA* 25 (1962), 98–120, on the leagues headed by ancient Damascus.

Moreover, the very problem the hypothesis seeks to answer, the combination of new tribes entering Canaan after the exodus or experiences with groups already settled in the land and without these experiences, need not be real. There is no reason to doubt that the two (or more) groups shared common traditions of a nomadic past, a common culture, at least in general as compared with that of the true Canaanites, and certain religious affinities (be it only the use of a common divine name as opposed again to those used in Canaanite religion).[21] Why should it be difficult for such groups to unite and accept the experiences of the new-comers as manifestations of the might of their common god? Even the passionate loyalty to the idea of the whole group detected by J. Dus[22] could be explained on this basis. Tribal affinities can be very strong! However, frankly such passionate loyalty to the whole does not seem to me particularly characteristic of the world of the judges.

Treaty Texts and Covenant Texts

First, what of developments in the study of ancient treaties themselves? No new texts of importance have been published apart from the fragmentary treaties of the Hittites with the Kaskaeans.[23] These are further examples of the flexibility of the form. They may also help with a problem: the role of the men listed as witnesses in certain treaty texts. Such lists of human endorsers pertain to the genre of the contract, not that of the oath with its divine witnesses, to which the treaty belongs. Human witnesses came into play when a treaty was restored or altered. They function as witnesses to the authenticity of the new document, not to the treaty relationship itself.[24]

---

[21] For details of the nomadic traditions see Buccellati, *Cities of Syria*, 89–90: for the general cultural unity of the Hebrews, Orlinsky, 'Tribal System', and Schmitt, *Landtag*, 92–3. Buccellati's argument, 235, based on the fragmentation produced by nomadic invasions of organized states elsewhere, e.g., the Ur III empire, as opposed to the unity the Israelites achieved amid the fragmented and fragmentizing Canaanite culture they invaded, strongly points up the original unity of the newcomers, whether they came in one or many waves.

[22] 'Die altisraelitische amphiktyonische Poesie', *ZAW* 75 (1963), 45–54.

[23] E. von Schuler, *Die Kaškäer*, Berlin, 1965.

[24] Cf. E. von Schuler, 'Staatsverträge und Dokumente hethitischen Rechts', *Historia, Einzelschriften* 7, Wiesbaden, 1964, 34–53.

There is an excellent new edition of the Aramaic treaties from Sefire to accompany Dupont-Sommer's *editio princeps*.[25] V. Korošec has studied the treaties as an integral part of cuneiform law. He finds that like so much of that law they constitute a fundamental continuity for more than two millennia before our era.[26] It becomes increasingly clear that treaty relationships were felt to be somehow familial. A treaty created 'brotherhood' and made 'fathers' and 'sons'. Semitic societies and their satellites seem to have seen all relationships as some kind of extension of their basic group, the family, and as in that relationship, they lasted over the generations (thus treaties did not automatically need renewal at the death of one party but could continue in force for the successor).[27]

The obligations of the overlord and their basis remain a vexed problem. Was he bound by oath? This is usually denied, but the position is becoming more difficult to maintain. We read that if the Hittite king's garrison among his vassal misbehaves, 'it breaks these oaths' (Treaty with Duppi-Teshub; cf. *ANET*, 205). This is the same language used for the misbehaviour of a vassal, and it is hard to deny that the Great King was bound by some kind of oath. A secular treaty in the Old Testament has the superior Israelites taking an oath to form a covenant with the miserable Gibeonites (Josh. 9:15). Finally, Liverani has shown that the vassal definitely felt his lord must help him, not as a grace but as a sacred obligation.[28] But note that the later Assyrian word for 'treaty', *ādē*, is said to be restricted to obligations laid by a superior on an inferior and sworn to only by the latter.[29] If so, this refers to one kind of treaty, and is an interesting parallel to one meaning of the Hebrew *berît*, i.e., obligation imposed on another, according to Kutsch's analysis. However, it should be emphasized that, while we have many examples of the word *ādē*,

[25] J. Fitzmyer, S.J., *The Aramaic Inscriptions of Sefire*, *Biblica et orientalia* 19, Rome, 1967.

[26] 'Keilschriftrecht', *Handbuch der Orientalistik*, 1. *Abteilung*, *Ergänzungsband* III; *Orientalisches Recht*, Leiden, 1964, 198–202. See also J. A. Thompson, *The Ancient Near Eastern Treaties and the Old Testament*, London, 1963, for a survey confined to international treaties.

[27] Buccellati, *Cities of Syria*, 68, 86: Korošec, ibid.

[28] 'Contrasti e confluenze . . .', *Revue d'assyriologie* 61 (1967), 1–18.

[29] See I. Gelb, review of Wiseman, *The Vassal Treaties of Esarhaddon*, in *Bibliotheca orientalis* 19 (1962), 159–62.

it is hard to find any examples of *parity dealings* in later Assyrian history when it was used, so that we cannot be sure what they were called. In other words, the restricted meaning of *ādē* depends largely on an *argumentum ex silentio*.

A possible Hittite parallel to the David-Goliath story is another example of the affinities between Asia Minor and the Levant, or better the unity of the whole eastern Mediterranean world.[30] In the study of Assyrian-Philistine relations we can see the treaty system at work. It attempts to achieve a secure relationship not by brute force but by varied and appropriate dealings; e.g., the restoration of a rebellious vassal, something the horrific curses of the treaty documents would not lead us to expect.[31]

Some of the reactions to the actual application of the treaty form to the study of biblical texts are rather well exemplified in the Jubilee Volume of the Society for Old Testament Study, *Archaeology and Old Testament Study*.[32] Professor Wiseman has considered and rejected my arguments against attributing a treaty form to the Sinai covenant,[33] while Professor Gray lists the various possibilities and leaves the question open.[34] If we add S. B. Frost's paper, which can discuss the problem of Josiah's death, the theology of retribution, and a Deuteronomic context without notice of the studies of the treaty character of Israel's covenant, and particularly Deuteronomy,[35] it seems that we have almost covered the range of reactions. The final option is to list only those applications which support one's own opinion.[36] It seems to me that methodologically the last two are hard to justify. The question is open and much discussed. In the circumstances one is entitled to take a firm position, but not by ignoring the whole question or at least disagreement on the point.

A survey of this range of opinions about the place of the treaty form as a means of expressing Israel's relation to Yahweh can begin with the simplest: the denial of the usage or at least of its

[30] H. A. Hoffner, Jr., 'A Hittite Analogue to the David and Goliath Contest of Champions?', *CBQ* 30 (1968), 220–5.
[31] H. Tadmor, 'Philistia under Assyrian Rule', *BA* 29 (1966), 86–102.
[32] Ed. D. Winton Thomas, Oxford, 1967.
[33] Ibid., 132, n. 10.   [34] Ibid., 164, n. 55.
[35] 'The Death of Josiah: A Conspiracy of Silence', *JBL* 87 (1968), 369–82.
[36] E.g., W. Beyerlin, *Hertzberg Festschrift*, 25–9.

relevance. A. Jepsen argues that the Nash Papyrus (second century B.C.) assimilates the Exodus Decalogue to that in Deuteronomy, and this is but a further step in the process already visible in MT''s Exodus. Carrying form history a step farther back, we arrive at a combination of forms: a divine address (*Jahwewort*) expressing God's attitude towards Israel, and a prophetic address summing up the norms of human conduct under this God. This has nothing to do with treaties or apodictic law. It defines the basic relation of Israel and Yahweh in its own right [37] H. Gese is not sure about the external parallel to the treaties, but he thinks it is immaterial in any case. Sinai and its covenant were essentially matters of cult. When they were treated as history in connection with the story of the Exodus, it was a remarkable example of 'secularization', uniting the sacred to the profane, a religious insight which had nothing to do with the Hittite practice of attaching historical material to all kinds of documents, not only or especially to treaties.[38]

On the other hand, many find the parallel between the Sinai stories and the treaties convincing. E. W. Nicholson sees this as pointing to a covenant ceremony with a structure like that of the book of Deuteronomy, following in this, of course, von Rad and J. J. Stamm.[39] Very recently D. Hillers has published *Covenant: The History of a Biblical Idea*,[40] based on the theories first elaborated by Mendenhall. He recognizes development and a fruitful tension between different ideas of covenant (e.g., the Mosaic and the Davidic), and his presentation is carefully nuanced. This is an eminently worthwhile book, but one to be read with the *caveat* that it builds upon a hypothetical form of the Mosaic covenant which is open to disagreement.

It is not really clear where K. Koch stands on the whole question. He accepts the treaty parallel. He connects it with a cove-

[37] 'Beiträge zur Auslegung und Geschichte des Dekalogs', *ZAW* 79 (1968), 277–304. I shall not discuss the immense literature on the Decalogue as such: J. J. Stamm and M. E. Andrew, *The Ten Commandments in Recent Research*, Studies in Biblical Theology 2/2, London, 1967, offers a thorough survey which improves the German original by including much more material, particularly in the area of possible relations of apodictic law and the treaty form.
[38] 'Bemerkungen zur Sinaitradition', *ZAW* 79 (1967), 137–54.
[39] *Deuteronomy and Tradition*, Oxford, 1967, 43–5.
[40] Baltimore, 1969.

nant renewal festival. However, he notes differences between the treaties and the Israelite covenant formulary. For example, he says that Israel takes no oath to serve Yahweh as his vassal.[41] This is rather mystifying, since most who defend the vassal treaty view of the covenant make a point of oath or acceptance, in both the rite and the record of covenant (cf. Exod. 24:3-8; Deut. 26:16-18; Josh. 24:14-24). Neither is it clear where in the liturgical calendar Koch would place the covenant renewal feast, nor does he specify when it came into use. Does the covenant in treaty form go back to Moses, or is it a later development?

J. Muilenburg sees the treaty form as the background for the judgments preached by the northern (Israelite rather than Judean) prophets. While he does not want to insist over much on the cult, he thinks that these prophets knew the covenant in this form principally from its use in the cult. They may sometimes even have been cult officers.[42] This argues to a cult which preserved a concept of covenant in treaty form and antedated the prophets. Does it go back to Moses in essentials?

A growing number of authors seem to doubt the early date for the form, if not the existence of the form itself in the Old Testament. For E. Nielsen it is a late adaptation which turned the Decalogue into a document with an historical introduction and a set of stipulations on the model of the treaty.[43] G. Fohrer sees a growth from the idea of kinship with the deity in the patriarchal covenants. In Canaan Israel's situation was so different from its beginning that this and every thought of covenant died out. Hence the lack of concern for covenant in the prophets. A new stage began with the Deuteronomic reform. Covenant reappears as the thing which makes Israel God's people. Fohrer sees this as an influence from politics, for he follows Frankena in taking Deuteronomy as an adaptation of an Assyrian treaty to a

---

[41] *The Growth of the Biblical Tradition*, New York, 1969, 31-2, 196, n. 4.

[42] 'The "Office" of the Prophet in Ancient Israel', *The Bible in Modern Scholarship*, ed. by J. Philip Hyatt, Nashville, Tenn., 1965, 89-97.

See also H. J. Kraus, *Worship in Israel*, Oxford, 1966, 101-13, for a fuller discussion of the prophet who is supposed to have represented Moses as proclaimer of law at festivals: followed by E. M. Good, 'Hosea 5:8-6:6: An Alternative to Alt', *JBL* 85 (1966), 273-86.

[43] *The Ten Commandments in New Perspective, Studies in Biblical Theology* 2/7, London, 131, 143.

religious expression. The climax of growth is reached when P sees all history as a sequence of covenants, emphasizing not kinship with God but his absolute sovereignty,[44] R. Martin-Achard, though he puts added importance on the covenant meal, seems quite sympathetic to Fohrer's view.[45] Julius Wellhausen probably would be too! And I do not mean this simply as a joke. We often seem in danger of forgetting the importance of development, and the great pioneer can always remind us of it to our profit.

Another study done by P. Buis emphasizes development. He rightly demands care in defining the covenant formulary (*Bundesformular*, K. Baltzer's name for the Israelite adaptation of treaty). This restricts him practically to three texts, Exod. 19:3–8; Josh. 24:1–13; and Exod. 23:20–6. He believes that Israel could have become acquainted with the form only when as a state under the kings it became involved in international law. Despite this origin its real setting was in the Levitical preaching. It was an artful adaptation for parenetic purposes, since it did not involve a real conception of a vassal relationship to Yahweh because, according to Buis, the overlord never obligated himself to his vassal, while on the contrary, the central concept of Israelite faith was that Yahweh had bound himself by promise to his people.[46]

H. Cazelles cautiously suggests that Deuteronomy used the form to express the heritage of prophets like Hosea.[47] Perhaps he would alter the view or go further because of his partial acceptance of G. Minette de Tillesse's analysis of the variation between the singular and the plural of the second person in Deuteronomy.[48] In essence, Minette[49] sees the plural passages as a later Deuteronomistic introduction of the idea of rewards or punishments which are conditioned on obedience. This is a necessary element in the

[44] 'Das sogenannte apodiktisch formulierte Recht und der Dekalog', *Kerygma und Dogma* 11 (1965), 49–74: 'AT—"Amphiktyonie" und "Bund"', *TLZ* 91 (1966), 802–16, 893–904.

[45] 'La signification de l'Alliance dans l'Ancien Testament d'après quelques travaux récents', *Revue de théologie et de philosophie*, 3rd series, 18 (1968), 88–102.

[46] P. Buis, 'Les formulaires d'Alliance', *VT* 16 (1966), 396–411.

[47] 'Pentateuque', *Supplément au Dictionnaire de la Bible* VI, Paris, 1964, col. 762.

[48] 'Passages in the Singular within Discourses in the Plural of Dt. 1–4', *CBQ* 29 (1967), 207–19.

[49] 'Sections "tu" et sections "vous" dans le Deutéronome', *VT* 12 (1962), 29–87.

treaty form. It is, of course, also the element which under prophetic guidance is seen to work out Israel's destiny in the
Deuteronomistic review of history, and the Deuteronomistic
school might have wished to point it up in Deuteronomy, its
guidebook, so to speak.

R. Frankena makes Deuteronomy the expression of the Josian
reform. It is the transposition of a treaty such as had tied Judah
to Assyria as a vassal state. The change makes Yahweh the overlord and the people his proud vassals. The stipulations, of course,
are very different from those of an Assyrian political treaty, but
the underlying concept of the relationship is the same. So is the
form, as Frankena shows by a number of correspondences in
detail between Deuteronomy and Assyrian treaties.[50] Note that
Frankena is not simply renewing the long-exploded theory that
Deuteronomy was a 'forgery' made up to serve Josiah's purposes
of religio-political reform. The treaty form may have been a
relatively new mode of expression, but in many things it was a
return to old Israelite ideas in new dress.

Finally, M. Weinfeld sees Deuteronomy as the typical expression of the treaty form in the Old Testament. It uses detailed
borrowings from or imitations of the language and imagery of
the treaties.[51] So sophisticated a means of expression could only
have come from learned official circles, that is, from the scribes
of the royal entourage. This is substantiated by the frequency of
wisdom themes in Deuteronomy.[52] In thus expressing Israel's
relation with its God in terms of his sovereignty the scribes of
Hezekiah and Josiah (for such an effort could have come only
from times of religious revival) gave Israel '. . . a religio-national
ideology inspired by the sapiential-didactic school. They freed
Israelite faith from its mythical character, religious worship from
its ritual stress, and the laws of the Torah from their strict
legalistic character'.[53]

If this survey accurately reflects current thought, it seems to

[50] R. Frankena, 'The Vassal-Treaties of Esarhaddon and the Dating of
Dt', *Oud-Testamentische Studien* 14 (1965), 122–54.
[51] 'Traces of Assyrian Treaty Formulae in Deuteronomy', *Biblica* 46
(1965), 417–27.
[52] Already discussed in my *Treaty and Covenant*, c. 9, and J. Malfoy,
'Sagesse et loi dans le Deutéronome', *VT* 15 (1965), 49–65.
[53] 'Deuteronomy—the Present State of Inquiry', *JBL* 86 (1967),
249–62.

me to show a healthy nuancing of the application of the treaty. Moreover, it has long been my contention that the parallel with the treaties is clearest in Deuteronomy and Deuteronomistic passages. Older concepts of the covenant between Yahweh and Israel were different, and the cultic element, as recognized by H. Gese, R. Martin-Achard, and others, was stressed. Nor was there a simple leap from one concept to a new one. There was rather development in which the older was not lost but subsumed in the new. The treaty parallel is not a cure-all, and we will understand a principal element in Old Testament religion to the degree that we see covenant in all its variety by letting each text speak to us on its own, and then trying to see the dialectic of the development of the idea and the institution.

Criticism of the Form-Critical Parallel: Treaty and Covenant

We have already seen the elements of most such criticism but it may be helpful to sum them up under a single rubric. First there are the students of the sociology of ancient Syria and Palestine. Liverani casts doubt on the vitality of the vassal principle, just at the moment, towards the end of the second millennium B.C., when it has been supposed to be most effective upon Israel, and he makes it seem unlikely that any group much influenced by Egypt would know or esteem it in any case. Buccellati and G. Schmitt (though the latter accepts a Mosaic treaty-type covenant) emphasize the cultural and natural unity of the tribes over against an artificial union by compact.

The section immediately preceding has shown that many, if not most, recent writers are unwilling to assert that the treaty form is to be found in the Sinai narratives. Some doubt that it was ever used, others connect it with the monarchy and Deuteronomy.

Perhaps most important are new ideas about the Decalogue, supposed to be the very charter of Israel's treaty covenant with Yahweh. A. Jepsen and E. Nielsen simply deny any connection, at least at an early stage of Israelite religion. For different reasons H. Cazelles does the same.[54] Positively, Gerstenberger first showed the connection of the precepts with clan wisdom and the late growth of collections as large as the Decalogue, all of which rules out an origin in the treaty form. W. Richter has also connected the precept or prohibition with the wisdom traditions

[54] *Supplément au Dictionnaire de la Bible* VII, col. 76.

which guided the leading classes in Israel.[55] E. Auerbach has tried
to defend an original form grouping precepts in tens, but his
arguments are not convincing in the face of Gerstenberger and
Richter.[56]

The Sinai Covenant and Shechem

The earlier discussion of covenant and institution applies here,
for Shechem is commonly considered the first centre for traditions of the Sinai–Horeb covenant. There have been efforts to
distinguish a northern tradition, based on the Mosaic covenant in
treaty form, from the southern, more influenced by royal ideology.[57] To some extent this might be supported by E. C. Kingsbury's analysis of the descriptions of theophanies into two
originally separate elements: the earthquake and the thunder-
storm. The latter is the older and it is northern. It characterizes
the E account of the Sinai event.[58] Thus E has the older picture
of the all-important Sinai experience, and it would be attached
to the north, but in itself this says nothing about the form of the
covenant.

M. Newman offers the most thorough study of contrasting
northern and southern conditions.[59] He reconstructs a tradition

[55] *Recht und Ethos, SANT* 15, Munich, 1955. Richter's insistence on a
distinction between a 'vetative' (*'al* + jussive) and a 'prohibitive' (*lo'* +
imperfect) seems artificially based on purely external criteria, and despite
K. Koch's objections to lumping together positive and negative commands of various external form (*Growth*, 9, n. 11) all of these, 'vetative',
'prohibitive', and command, are apodictic 'laws' designed to keep society
going and can (I think, must) be treated together as a common response
to a common situation: that is, as a valid 'literary' form (using 'literary'
here as a normal technical convention, since in fact here more often than
elsewhere we are dealing with matters at home in the everyday *talk* of
the people).
[56] 'Das Zehngebot—Allgemeine Gesetzes-Form in der Bibel', *VT* 16
(1966), 255–76.
[57] Cf. Muilenburg, n. 42, and J. Gray, *I and II Kings*, index *sub ver.*
'covenant'. Earlier Gray (cf. *VT* 4 (1954), 150) saw affinities between the
Sinai-Qadesh traditions and Zion theology. The positions are not
mutually exclusive, for if the north emphasized a particular view of the
Horeb covenant, the south certainly had its own view of Sinai.
[58] 'The Theophany *Topos* and the Mountain of God', *JBL* 86 (1967),
205–10.
[59] *The People of the Covenant: A Study of Israel from Moses to the
Monarchy*, London, 1965.

of covenant in treaty form (conditional) which originally centred around the shrine of the Ark at Shechem. He finds another tradition of an unconditional covenant (promise), perhaps centred on the shrine of the Tent of Meeting at Hebron. This latter covenant was between God and a dynasty of priests and only through them did it reach the people. Later it was taken over and moved to Jerusalem to be elaborated into the Davidic dynastic covenant. Newman's synthesis is suggestive, and it pulls together many data. It offers a plausible set of ideologies underlying part of Hebrew history. However, it involves too many hypotheses to have been generally accepted. One weakness touches especially on our topic: it is hard to show that the Ark was ever at Shechem. If it was, it did not stay long, for it was at Gilgal and Bethel, and it even acquired a temple at Shiloh during the relatively short period of the conquest and the judges. Nor, as we have seen, is there any solid evidence that it was the central cult object of a putative amphictyony anyway, for it plays no role in most of the major activity of the time, whether as part of the paraphernalia of worship or as palladium in war. Men offered sacrifices and fought their battles and no mention is made of it.

If the Ark were so important at Shechem, why has it no place in Josh. 24? This is the capital text for those who insist on the importance of Shechem in preserving a Mosaic covenant modelled on the treaties. For myself, I have reservations about the role Shechem played in developing Israel's religious traditions. Because Alt's great study of the origins of Hebrew law made much of the curse ceremony on Ebal in Deuteronomy 27, the text and the place have assumed an important role in studies of law and covenant. But clearly Deut. 27:14–26 is neither of these. It is a liturgical ceremony against those who have already broken the law, not a proclamation of law or a ratification of covenant.

Neither can Josh. 24:1–28 bear the weight put upon it. It is not easy to find the treaty form here.[60] In fact, as Noth long ago

[60] No two attempts to reconstruct the treaty pattern are the same: cf. my *Treaty and Covenant*, 147–8: E. M. Good, *JBL* 85 (1966), 285–6, adds another interpretation; the repeated affirmations of the people are some sort of formality, the first answer not being enough and needing the others to ratify their allegiance. He urges Hos. 5:15–6:6 and Exod. 24 3–8, as parallels, though they involve but two affirmations and in the first instance even the people's second answer is not accepted and in the second instance the first answer is enough.

pointed out, the whole 'historical prologue' (vv. 2–13) is irrele-
vant.[61] It does not really motivate the demand in v. 14 to put
aside the gods of Mesopotamia, since they have been forgotten
since v. 3. (The history itself puts the Amorite gods *hors de
combat* before the demand to put them aside is made.) The
language is largely Deuteronomistic (cf. M. Noth, *Josua*, in loc.).
V. 19 is unique. It may presume royal-priestly ideas ('holiness'),
the later parenetic elements of the Decalogue, and prophetic concepts of God's absolute dominion. The invocation of witnesses
(v. 22) belongs properly to the covenant, not to oath or treaty. It
is paralleled by the covenant renewal in Neh. 9:10. Considering
the language, the parallels, and especially the setting—a problem
with Mesopotamian gods—it is hard to see the text as reflecting
early conditions. Its problems are those of the later days of the
monarchy when Assyrian gods posed a temptation, or even of the
exilic era when Babylon's gods did (cf. Deutero-Isaiah's vigorous
polemic against them). I realize that this is a summary treatment
of a large problem, and I do not deny that Shechem played a large
role in Israel's early experience. However, there is not space for a
full treatment, and precisely because the text is so important it is

[61] *System der zwölf Stämme*, 69. Von Rad, of course, separates the 'historical prologue' from what follows in his famous study of the form for
the Hexateuch: Buis, *VT* 16 (1966), 396–411, also treats the historical
passage as separate for the interesting reason that *it* is the covenant formulary (*Bundesformular*) in this chapter. As was noted in the first part of
this survey, there is a growing tendency to question von Rad's separation
of the exodus from the Sinai traditions. In so far as this recognizes the
principle that the burden of proof is on one who wishes to make a major
alteration in the tradition as it comes to us in the text, there is much to be
said for it. However, the argument that the Sinai event was essentially a
ceremony and so not matter for historical narrative should not be pressed
by those who insist on the Hittite treaty form for Sinai. It was normal
practice in the Hittite treaties to make a point of citing previous treaties
with the party in question. If the 'little historical credo' is a reminiscence
of the historical prologue of the covenant repeated at covenant renewals
and the like, the analogy with the Hittite treaties would indicate that a
reference to the original covenant at Sinai would be *de rigueur* (cf. P. B.
Harner, 'Exodus, Sinai, and Hittite Prologues', *JBL* 85 (1966), 233–7).
It is worth noting also that L. Rost, 'Das kleine geschichtliche Credo',
Kleine Credo, 11–24, finds that the supposedly more primitive record of
this standard historical reminiscence, Deut. 26:5–10, is deuteronomistic
in its language. Perhaps a late date for the more elaborate form in Josh. 24
is not so unreasonable after all.

desirable to try to look at it with fresh eyes, even though the
glance be all too short.

Further Traces of the Covenant Form

Apart from the major texts, Exod. 19–24:24; Josh. 24; and
Deuteronomy, there are other texts which are said to display the
treaty or covenant form. This has been widely held of Exod.
19:3–8, for instance, and P. Buis sees another part of the Sinai
narrative as having the form, Exod. 23:20–6. The sending of
the angel mentioned in vv. 20–1 is an accomplished fact and so
an historical prologue. V. 22 defines the covenant, 23–5a are
its stipulations, and 25b–6 its blessings. Perhaps so, but it is not
easy to separate this section from the promise of help in the conquest, if the people are faithful. For instance, v. 23 is hardly a
stipulation. And why end the blessing with v. 26?[62]

Generally the claims do not find the whole of the form but
merely reflections of this or that part of it. W. Beyerlin wants
to explain the parenetic elements in the Covenant Code as an
application of the encouragement to fidelity found in the vassal
treaties.[63] Knowing itself Yahweh's vassal, Israel turned to this
kind of encouragement in the face of the temptations of Canaan.
Hence the parenesis can go back to the time of settlement and is
not due to Deuteronomic influence. One can accept the conclusion without the argument which assumes that a vassal treaty
between Yahweh and Israel is recorded at Sinai. This, of course,
wants proof, and it is as easy to imagine encouragement based on
duty to Yahweh the king of the tribes, Yahweh the warrior,
Yahweh the thunderer on the mountain, and many other things.

So it is with F. C. Fensham's reading of Ps. 21.[64] It involves a
blessing of the king and threats to his enemies, but surely this
could be done without benefit of a treaty. The operative word is
ḥesed in v. 8. It does mean covenant fidelity, but it can mean
marital fidelity as well in Hosea; hence fidelity in general, so that
by itself it does not prove the presence of a covenant or covenant
thinking.

When J. Wijngaards interprets the enigmatic dying and rising

[62] *VT* 16 (1966), 396–411.
[63] 'Die Paränese im Bundesbuch und ihre Herkunft', *Hertzberg Festschrift*, 9–29.
[64] 'Ps. 21—A Covenant Song', *ZAW* 77 (1965), 193–202.

of Israel in Hos. 6:1–2 in terms of ending and renewing covenant, one almost wishes he were right and another crux solved.[65]
However, he depends in part on the numbers '. . . after two days
. . . on the third day'. There is really nothing in the treaties
parallel to this. It is the familiar ancient figure of increasing numbers for emphasis.[66] 'To die' and 'to come alive' do belong to
treaty vocabulary, but as part of cuneiform legal language in
general. The metaphor is used for the invalidity and validity of
documents.[67]

The problem with all this sort of thing is that the parallels with
the treaties are possible, but other parallels are equally so. Here I
think that K. R. Veenhof's interpretation of a difficult passage in
the Sefire stelas might serve as a model.[68] He reads Sefire II C by
comparing it with building inscriptions, boundary stones, law
codes, etc. This is true form criticism, for it fixes the proper
setting, the protection of a valuable text, and reads the text in
terms of the way the ancients responded to the setting: by a
stereotyped set of curses. The point is that he establishes an
exclusive parallel, not simply one of several possibilities.

Some claims of the influence of the treaty form on the Bible
turn on details. After W. Moran, in an article in *JNES*, had
shown that Akkadian *ṭubtu u sulummu* is connected with treaties,
D. Hillers has found a reflex of this in the word *ṭôbâ* in Deut. 23:7
and 2 Sam. 2:6.[69] The first seems very likely: it corresponds to
the Deuteronomic rejection of alliances with gentiles near Palestine. The other is less convincing. Certainly David wanted to
have the good will of Jabesh-Gilead just as Saul had. But is there
any indication that the relationship was more than that? Specifically, that it included a treaty?

It is much the same with the equation of Hebrew *yd'* with the

[65] 'Death and Resurrection in Covenantal Context', *VT* 17 (1967),
226–39.
[66] E.g., in Amos 1:3–2:6: E. M. Good, *JBL* 85 (1968), 280, 285, sees
the three days of Hosea as referring to ritual purification as at Sinai
(Exod. 19:10).
[67] For documentation of the legal usage, see W. von Soden, *Akkadisches
Hand-Wörterbuch* under *balāṭu* and *mūtu*.
[68] 'An Aramaic Curse with a Sumero-Akkadian Prototype', *Bibliotheca
orientalis* 20 (1963), 142–4.
[69] 'A Note of Some Treaty Terminology in the Old Testament',
BASOR 176 (1964), 46–7 (see above, ch. 2, n. 12).

Akkadian *idū* of the treaties, where it means 'recognize (politically)' as well as 'serve faithfully'.[70] Perhaps Israel was called on to recognize Yahweh's lordship in an analogous sense and so to serve him. But *yd'* is a technical word in the liturgy and in wisdom circles with a very similar semantic field. As with *ṭôbâ,* each case must be studied carefully in its own right to find its true setting and exact import.

Covenant and the Prophets

Once more we can but touch a few examples from an immense literature. We have already noticed a tendency to connect the prophet with a covenant cult (cf. n. 42 of this postscript), but not all prophets were officers of a possible covenant feast. Did they still relate to the covenant and to a covenant in the treaty form? E. von Waldow, in his study of the tradition which formed the prophets, gives an unequivocal affirmative answer.[71] Hillers, as it seems to me, abandons the caution of his study of the prophets and the curse forms which showed that the prophets stood in a very general tradition in the imagery of their threats, not in one which was exclusive to the treaties. In any case, he now finds the prophetic message governed in large part by the demands of a vassal relationship to Yahweh.[72]

Probably the most important contribution in this area is J. Harvey's book on the covenant lawsuit.[73] It gives by far the fullest documentation on the whole question. He makes the point so often overlooked that the prophets, even when they used judicial forms, did not always condemn outright. Sometimes the proceedings issued in an admonition, a sort of probationary sentence in our idiom. Still, the basis for the specifically *covenantal* character of the lawsuit is rather narrow. The strong point in the argument is the appeal to the heavens and/or earth, which often occur as witnesses to the treaties. The biblical lawsuits would

[70] H. B. Huffmon, 'The Treaty Background of Hebrew *Yāda'*, *BASOR* 181 (1966), 31–7; and, with S. B. Parker, 'A Further Note on the Treaty Background of Hebrew *Yāda'*, ibid. 184 (1966), 36–8.

[71] *Der traditionsgeschichtliche Hintergrund der prophetischen Gerichtsreden, BZAW* 85, Berlin, 1963.   [72] *Covenant,* c. 6.

[73] *Le Plaidoyer prophétique contre Israel après la rupture de l'Alliance, Studia* 22, Paris and Montreal, 1967. E. M. Good, *JBL* 85 (1966), 284–5, supports the idea of a covenant lawsuit without committing himself as to its form. See also Hillers, *Covenant,* 129–31.

seem to show five examples: Isa. 1:2–3, 10–20; Jer. 2:4–12; Mic. 6:1–8; Ps. 50; and Deut. 32. However, the instance from Isaiah is weak. 1:2–3 contain the appeal, 1:10 ff. the lawsuit, and it is not clear that the two should be connected. Yet the lawsuit does occur, and it takes Israel to task for false worship, that is, for violating the basic condition of its relationship with Yahweh, however it is to be described and on whatever it was based.

The problem remains the exact relation of the lawsuit to covenant. Surely the prophets did not appeal to the highly specialized covenant suit alone. They apply the analogy of ordinary legal procedure in most of their contentions with a backsliding Israel.[74] The crux is the appeal to heaven and/or earth. Does it recall treaty usage? M. Delcor can see no other possibility.[75] However, J. R. Boston has studied all twelve invocations of the heavens and/or earth in the Old Testament. He concludes that there is so much variety in the usage, even within the so-called covenant lawsuits, that it cannot be too closely connected with a specific form.[76]

This is not to say that the prophets never used covenantal ideas as such. They probably did. W. Brueggemann makes a good case for describing their activity as the application of covenant traditions to new circumstances.[77] But it is not clear that these traditions could have been connected only with a covenant in treaty form.

Human Covenants in Israel

There is increasing evidence that Israel used something in the nature of treaties (not necessarily in 'treaty-form'!) in its political

[74] K. Koch, *Growth*, 220, n. 21, insists on the diversity in the use of the lawsuit analogy without being clear as to possible formal diversities which may be involved. F. Horst, 'Recht und Religion im Bereich des Alten Testament', *Gottes Recht*, 260–91, can explain most of the phenomena even of the covenant lawsuit in terms of ordinary legal procedure; B. Gemser, 'The *rîb* or Controversy-Pattern in Hebrew Mentality', *VT Suppl.* 3 (1955), 120–37, does so entirely.

[75] 'Les attachés litteraires, l'origine et la signification de l'expression biblique "Prendre à témoin le ciel et la terre" ', *VT* 16 (1966), 8–25.

[76] 'The Wisdom Influence upon the Song of Moses', *JBL* 87 (1968), 198–202.

[77] *Tradition for Crisis: A Study in Hosea*, Richmond, Va., 1968.

dealings. Even before the monarchy this appears in the Gibeon episode: historical references (Jos. 9:9–11), stipulation and oath (by the superior! Josh. 9:15), and eating together (Josh. 9:14), all of which are represented in treaty-making of one sort or another.[78]

Hanna Kassis suggests that 1 Kgs. 2:39–40 and David's Gittite bodyguard reveal a treaty between Israel and Gath. It would have offered internal autonomy, military protection, and access to Judean trade (compare the trade agreements between Israel and Damascus in Ahab's time) to Gath in return for the 600-man bodyguard and a tribute of produce.[79] He fails to mention 1 Kgs. 2:41, which reveals a quasi-universal part of the treaty demands: the delivery of fugitives by the vassal to the overlord.

F. C. Fensham thinks there may have been a treaty between Israel and the Kenites. 1 Sam. 15:6 calls on the Kenites to avoid fighting on the side of Amalek (perhaps even to join against it) because of the *ḥesed* between them and Israel, and *ḥesed* and military co-operation are often related to treaties. Jael the Kenite's murder of Sisera (Judg. 4:17–22; 5:24–7) would reflect the treaty principle: 'Your friend is my friend, your enemy is my enemy'.[80]

Covenant and Kingship

This rubric includes discussions of the promissory covenants with the patriarchs, for these latter share with the royal covenant a special character precisely as covenants. They are unconditioned promises of an enduring relationship. Further, R. E.

---

[78] Cf. J. Blenkinsopp, 'Are there Traces of the Gibeonite Covenant in Deuteronomy?', *CBQ* 28 (1966), 213–14. J. M. Grintz, 'The Treaty of Joshua with the Gibeonites', *JAOS* 86 (1966), 113–26, has a far more elaborate description, but it is vitiated by insisting on a one-for-one correspondence with the Hittite treaties and their social situations, but the problem of what the correspondences were, how far they went, and how they came about is far too complex and obscure to allow this sort of application of the connection.

[79] *JBL* 84 (1965), 269.

[80] 'Did a Treaty between the Israelites and the Kenites Exist?' *BASOR* 175 (1964), 51–4. One can explain all these facts by means of the common assumption that the Kenites were in fact Hebrews or at least very closely related to them and that the Hebrews recognized this.

All the examples cited in the text relate to Palestinian affairs. In a larger field K. Veenhof has explained the mechanics of the 'Treaty by oil' with Egypt (Hos. 12:2) which had puzzled me. Cf. ch. 4, n. 2.

Clements has recently made a strong case for a real connection between the form of the covenant with Abraham and that with David.[81]

In the first edition of this book I noted that the renewed interest in covenant had produced comparatively little study of the covenant with Abraham. This is no longer true. R. Kilian has produced a detailed study of the whole Abraham tradition. It spends much time on source analysis, but the work on Gen. 15 directly concerns our topic. Kilian finds the covenant ratification to be the essential feature of J in that chapter, and he considers J the basic stratum to which later redactors added. In his view of the larger whole, the chapter is part of J's development of the theme of God's justice in giving Abraham a promised heir. It moves towards the fulfilment in the birth of Isaac by making Abraham more than a mere receiver of a gift. He is now a partner of Yahweh by covenant.[82]

Kilian's approach absolves him from concern with the exact nature of the covenant in question, but his presentation does occasion a question. Our modern languages customarily use covenant (or *Bund* or *alliance*) of Israel's relation to Yahweh where the Bible does not use $b^e r\hat{\imath}t$. Is this legitimate? Or must we separate divine promises (usually expressed by a form of *dbr*) from the category of covenant? It seems legitimate to consider a sure promise as a covenant. After all, the Old Testament had no single necessary form for expressing or making covenants. The essential thing seems to have been that an obligatory relationship was formed. This is true even if we were to accept fully Kutsch's contention that $b^e r\hat{\imath}t$ means 'obligation'. An obligation is *to* someone or *between* parties, that is, it necessarily involves a relationship. Surely a promise from God was a firm basis for obligation, a fixed relationship we may still call covenant. So also of a divine command: it put an obligatory relationship upon the one commanded. But if Kilian is correct in thinking that the $b^e r\hat{\imath}t$ of Gen. 15 was somehow a source of greater dignity for Abraham, it seems that we should conclude that $b^e r\hat{\imath}t$, while not different in kind from other assumed or imposed obligatory relationships, was different in degree or in dignity.

[81] *Abraham and David, Studies in Biblical Theology* 2/5, London, 1967.
[82] *Die vorpriesterlichen Abrahamsüberlieferung, Bonner Bibel-Studien* 24, Bonn, 1966, 36–73, 295–99.

But to return to Gen. 15: N. Lohfink has offered a very different analysis.[83] Avoiding source criticism, he sees it as a remoulding of three salvation oracles (1–4: promise of a son; 5: promise of numerous descendants; 7–21: promise of possessing the land) into a kind of narrative. This artificial narrative was incorporated *en bloc* into J with the rather unwieldy explanatory additions of vv. 3 and 13–16 included to fit it into the larger story. This form-critical approach avoids the immense complexity involved in all attempts at source analysis of the chapter. It also gives an '*Urform*' of the Abraham covenant, promising possession of the land (Gen. 15:17), which Lohfink locates at the oak of Moreh near Shechem (cf. Gen. 12:6–7).

This fits rather well into certain aspects of Clements' study (cf. n. 81 in this section) of the relation between the Abraham and the Davidic covenants. He too finds elements of an oracle of salvation in Gen. 15:1–6. In vv. 7–12, 17–18a J develops this into a covenant promising possession of the land. Clements, however, goes on to point to the central importance of Hebron in the Abraham cycle. When we note that the name of the place is related to *ḥeber*, 'associate', and gather together the indications of a league centred there—it was the main town for Judah, Caleb, the Kenites and others—it is not difficult to conclude that this was the centre which cultivated the tradition of the promissory covenant with the patriarch Abraham. Then it is noted that Hebron was David's first real power base. He was a Judean and surely knew the traditions associated with the tribal centre. Finally, the covenant with Yahweh which established his dynasty was formally identical with the promissory covenant of Abraham. It is hard to escape the belief that the Davidic covenant built on the Abraham covenant tradition.[84]

Thus Clements suggests a continuity between the Hebron traditions of Abraham and the later covenant of David's dynasty. Others have been interested in the Davidic covenant in itself.

[83] *Die Landesverheissung als Eid*, Stuttgarter Bibelstudien 28, Stuttgart 1967.

[84] Clements acknowledges his debt to Newman's study of southern traditions centred at Hebron (cf. n. 59). In view of this evidence that the promissory covenant was at home in Palestine, if not native there, it is interesting that Abimilki, king of Tyre, speaks of a vassal's relations with his lord in terms which recall those of Nathan's oracle (Amarna Letter No. 147, lines 45–51: cf. *ANET*, 484).

T. E. Fretheim emphasizes the connection with Yahweh's choice of Zion.[85] In itself this was not a theological problem, but the emphasis on the choice of the Davidids and of the people only through them came in conflict with the Deuteronomic (and Sinaitic) view of the covenant with all the people as equals.[86] Hence the limitations on the kings in Deut. 17:14-20. Hillers also sees a tension between the Sinaitic and Davidic covenants. This was even felt but consciously ignored in David's prayer of response to Nathan's oracle. Moreover, Hillers thinks that the more or less private royal liturgy could not have had a large part in the religious life of the people. Perhaps by implicitly replacing the explicitly conditional character of the Sinaitic covenant, the royal covenant played its part in the development of Old Testament religion. Even so, the basic tension remained, so that, while the Deuteronomistic history could absorb the covenant with Abraham, it gives only grudging acknowledgement to the Davidic covenant.[87]

A rather more positive view of the royal covenant appears in T. C. G. Thornton and R. E. Clements.[88] The problem with the

[85] 'The Ark in Deuteronomy', *CBQ* 30 (1968), 1-14: oddly his argument depends on taking Ps. 132 as a relatively early picture of a liturgical procession of the Ark (cf. his 'Psalm 132: A Form Critical Study', *JBL* 86 (1967), 289-300), and in the same issue of *CBQ* D. Hillers, 'Ritual Procession of the Ark in Ps. 132?', 48-55, casts doubts on the view that the psalm speaks of a procession at all!

[86] This hardly gives sufficient importance to the role of Moses, particularly in J, but also in E. In both he is very definitely mediator of covenant, and it is possible to argue that Exod. 34:10 (J) points to a covenant with him and only through him with the people.

[87] *Covenant*, 110-19, 154-6: see also J. A. Soggin, 'Zur Entwicklung des alttestamentlichen Königtums', *Theologische Zeitschrift* 15 (1959), 401-18. The contention of Hillers that the Sinaitic covenant was clearly and explicitly conditional is not to be accepted without reservation.

[88] Thornton, 'Charismatic Kingship in Israel and Judah', *JTS* n.s. 14 (1963), 1-11, to be read in conjunction with A. Alt, 'The Settlement of the Israelites in Palestine', 'The Formation of the Israelite State in Palestine', and 'The Monarchy in the Kingdoms of Israel and Judah', *Essays in OT History*, 173-335; R. E. Clements, *God and Temple. The Idea of the Divine Presence in Ancient Israel*, Oxford, 1965. I do not mean that Thornton and Clements have identical things to say, but in summary they hold much that is alike. Clements, of course, has a much fuller discussion, and, to speak impressionistically, he seems to treat the Nathan oracle as somehow more of a reality. S. B. Frost, 'The Death of Josiah: A Conspiracy of Silence', *JBL* 87 (1968), 370, calls the covenant with the Davidids '. . . a

monarchy, in this view, was not its theological or social ortho-
doxy. It was more the shock of change from a loose league to a
centralized government. In the ancient Near East, it is true, the
king was very close to the gods. But this need not have been a
problem in Israel, for the king's role was complementary to
God's. He was the earthly representative of the divine. And just
as the king was next to God in leadership, so the palace would be
next to the temple, the vice-gerent dwelling next to the building
symbolizing the presence of the real ruler. It is in the light of all
this that we are to read Nathan's oracle. It is a kind of charter
declaring the legitimacy of David's rule, proclaiming the dynastic
covenant, and explaining the origins and role of the temple.[89]
Hence Buccellati can argue strongly against calling monarchy in
Israel an 'anomaly' (cf. J. Pedersen, *Israel* I–II, 23). It was rather
a necessary response to a social need. It was theologically
acceptable as '. . . an extension of the covenant *idea* for different
political leadership. The covenant corresponds to the demands of
Israelite, not of Canaanite consciousness. . . .' It was not, therefore, an imposition of Jebusite or other alien ideas.[90]

But what was the intrinsic nature of the Davidic covenant? De
Vaux has shown that the Hebrew king had all the characteristics
of a vassal in regard to Yahweh, an idea corresponding perfectly
with the view of kingship as the complement of divine rule.[91]
Now P. Calderone has studied Nathan's oracle, 2 Sam. 7:8–16,
from the specific point of view of the vassal treaty.[92] He finds

codicil, as it were, to a major covenant of Yahweh with the people . . .',
but he seems to hold that the really basic idea of Israelite religion was a
theology of retribution which he does not relate to covenant.

[89] Cf. Clements, *God and Temple*, 60.

[90] *Cities of Syria*, 211–12; see also 240–2; there is an extensive bibliography on the social background to the emergence of Hebrew kingship on
p. 82, nn. 19–20.

[91] Père de Vaux seems to feel that I disagree with him more than I do
(cf. *RB* 74 (1967), 286): his analysis is substantially correct. It stands even
without parallel with vassalship based on treaty, which seems unproven.
The anointing of the king borrowed from Egyptian ritual symbolized this
status sufficiently by itself (on this see now Clements, *Abraham and
David*, 49).

[92] *Dynastic Oracle and Suzerainty Treaty*, Logos 1, Manila, 1966. A.
Caquot, 'La prophétie de Nathan et ses échos lyriques', *VT Suppl.* 9
(1963), 213–24, has also treated the oracle, taking it as a unit designed to
emphasize the connection of the dynasty and temple and the importance

elements which appear in the treaties: historical references, the king's 'great name', the linking of general prosperity with that of the vassal king, a promise of dynastic succession, the concept of vassalship and sonship, and the demand for obedience from the vassal dynasty. However, important elements are also missing. One would expect notice of the previous elevation of the vassal to the throne, a demand of obedience from the vassal, David, himself, and conditional blessing and curses. Without these, and with the other elements appearing in peculiar ways and out of normal sequence, Calderone correctly denies a formal relationship between oracle and ·treaty. Rather there is a cluster of ideas which *taken together* are paralleled only in the vassal treaties. The similarities are conceptual, not formal.

In summary, it is impossible to bring all the interpretations of the various covenants together under one definition or a simple linear line of development. There are problems in the relation of the promise to Abraham with the covenant with him. There are problems in the relation of the Abraham covenant with the Davidic. Most of all, there are problems in the relation of the Sinaitic and the Davidic covenants. Surely this is in part due to our failure to understand, but it is also evidence of the vital complexity in our texts.

---

of both. Such a piece must stem from Jersualem and be related to the royal and Zion psalms. Caquot points especially to Ps. 89 which, with its use of mythological motifs (vv. 6–15), reveals an origin in circles which cultivated the royal ideology derived from Canaan. In it the dynasty is assigned a *berît*, a word lacking in the prophetic oracle. He sees this as a conscious verbal (no more) link with the Sinaitic covenant. He would seem to be thinking of a sort of royalist propaganda designed to make use of the covenant mystique. Delcor, *VT* 16 (1966), 17–19, on the other hand, thinks the mention of sun and moon (vv. 37–8) may be a subtle allusion via the invocations of natural phenomena in the treaties to a very real, formal covenant between Yahweh and David's dynasty. This is but a hint at the uncertainties we meet in these matters. For another, there is Caquot's interpretation of Ps. 132 as later and deuteronomic in atmosphere (not style) because it plays down the royal role (see also E. Kutsch, *ZAW* 79 (1967), 32), while Fretheim, *JBL* 86 (1967), 298, n. 43, thinks it must be much earlier than Ps. 89 because only as the royal covenant gradually gained ascendancy over the Sinaitic did the conditional element found in Ps. 132 fade into the background.

Covenant and Theology

In recent years there has been no attempt at a synthesis of Old
Testament theology around the concept of covenant which
approaches the magnitude of Eichrodt's *Theology of the Old
Testament*. The best survey is Hiller's *Covenant: The History of
a Biblical Idea*, which traces a certain view of covenant through
the Old Testament and even into the Qumran documents and the
New Testament. It shows great learning and an appreciation of
the complexities involved, but it is essentially a high-level popu-
larization. In the nature of the case, then, to be understood it
must avoid debate on points which are in fact disputed among
scholars. It must proceed in terms of a consistent and scholarly
respectable answer. Even with this limitation, it is a stimulating
book which should encourage theologians to work out the synthesis which our present state of knowledge allows and even
demands. [93]

F. C. Fensham has what may be called a programmatic article
for a covenant-based theology: 'Covenant, Promise and Expectation in the Bible'. [94] He sees the history of the Old Testament as
essentially a history of covenants. (He is another who finds that
the Davidic covenant complements rather than conflicts with
older ones.) These committed God to a series of promises, but
also entailed the possibility of curse if man failed to respond to
the divine initiative. In fact, the promises were only partially fulfilled because man's infidelity impeded them. Yet each failure
paradoxically carried with it new hopes. For example, the in-
adequacies of the Davidic dynasty encouraged Messianism.
However, as Fensham sees it, there was always a problem since
covenant involved law and so, inevitably, curse. This is particularly acute for Fensham because he seems to equate all covenants
with those in the treaty form and cannot give due weight to the
promissory covenants with Abraham and David. In any case, in
the end Jesus took upon himself the curse men had called down
upon themselves, overcame it, and established the new and en-

[93] I have not been able to see J. Feiner and M. Lohrer, edd., *Mys-
terium salutis* II which, according to S. Loersch, *Deuteronomium und seine
Auslegung*, 103, makes use of covenant concepts to construct a systematic
theology.

[94] *Theologische Zeitschrift* 23 (1967), 305–22.

during covenant of grace, the last stage of God's covenant-making with man (cf. Hillers, *Covenant*, 179–87, for a similar view). The idea is suggestive, and, by confronting the problem of relation between the Testaments, it brings covenant theology into touch with the currently burning hermeneutical question.

On a more modest scale R. E. Clements traces the workings of various concepts of covenant on the development of Old Testament literature. J uses the scheme of promise and fulfilment built on Abraham's covenant and culminating in David's empire as the guideline for his theological history. Deuteronomy and the Deuteronomistic school also go back to the promissory covenant, but they give primacy to the Sinai-Horeb covenant. In the promissory covenants they eliminate the royal elements while emphasizing Yahweh's oath to the patriarchs. On the other hand P had to confront the breakdown of the Deuteronomic concept of covenant, since the words of the prophets and the fall of Jerusalem had shown that its curses were fulfilled, that is, that the covenant had ended. So P took the opposite tack. The school turned again to the promissory covenant with Abraham but qualified it as eternal (*'ad 'ōlām*), a phrase and a concept taken from royal ideology. Because Sinai had been indelibly stamped with the Deuteronomic view of covenant by this time, P does not treat it as a covenant at all but rather as the fulfilment of the promissory covenant made with the patriarchs. From all this it is evident that the concept of covenant is not univocal.[95] The problem is whether the interplay of so many diverse ideas is to be fruitful or stultifying.

J. L'Hour concentrates on the ethical aspects of covenant theology.[96] The historical prologue, which he finds characteristic of almost all Old Testament covenant, establishes the absolute priority of God's choice of Israel. The Old Testament ethic, therefore, is one of response. It demands loyalty and justice, but emphasizes man's liberty. Because of this man can join with God in working out the course of history, for it is up to his choice whether blessing or curse will become operative. R. Martin-Achard criticizes this view because it fails to take into account the historical development of the covenant idea.[97] Further, it

[95] *Abraham and David*, 47–60, 67–77.
[96] *La morale de l'Alliance, Cahiers de la Revue biblique* 5, Paris, 1966.
[97] *Revue de théologie et de philosophie*, 3rd series 18 (1968), 101.

seems to me, it confines Old Testament ethic too much to the covenant context. We do better justice to the richness of the Old Testament ethic if we allow for the independent working of the wisdom tradition with its awe before the mystery of God and creation (e.g., Job 28), of the cult with its direct experience of the divine and of community, of the mere majesty of Yahweh, and so on. Any or all of these could call forth responses like those L'Hour claims for covenant. It is hardly true that in fact it was covenant alone which did call them forth, and these different motives would give their own colour to the responses.

We may fairly conclude that we do not yet have anything like an adequate theology of covenant. Further work should help to solve the problem of the relation between the Testaments in detail. It should also take more account of the diversity of covenant. For instance, if the covenant with Yahweh was celebrated at great feasts and knowledge of it handed down through them, this is not simply an historical fact. It offers a chance to learn something of how covenant was actually felt, the affective response it called forth in community and individual, which is a real part of its total meaning and significance. We know now that the medium is the message!

There is more. The cult was not merely a medium which handed on knowledge of the covenant as a relationship and a doctrine. Covenant was originally ratified and at least occasionally renewed by ritual action. That is, cult was constitutive of covenant so that its special meaning and effects must have affected the essential nature and meaning of covenant. Then, at a later stage, covenant was also constituted by some sort of oath ('giving one's word'; cf. Deut. 26:16–18). What did this mean for the connotations of covenant, and how did it relate to the cultic element which continued to be part of covenant? How did the interaction between the two ways of making covenant affect its real, that is, its affective as well as conceptual, meaning? Then there is the variety of covenant forms. How do they and the tensions they create affect the total concept of covenant?

Finally, we must take seriously the fact that wisdom traditions and priestly *torah* were independent and vital elements in the life of Israel. They influenced the concept and expression of covenant, and vice versa, but they did not absorb one another. We constantly try to reduce matters to an easily handled unity. We can do so only by excluding or oversimplifying things. A true appreciation of covenant in all its richness must recognize the variety within the covenant traditions themselves. It must also try to understand their relation to and interaction with other traditions without subsuming (and, in effect, transforming) them into covenant.

Bibliography

The following list of books and articles is arranged in the manner of the Bibliography in my *Treaty and Covenant*, *Analecta biblica* 21, Rome, 1963. It is not exhaustive, but it does include reference to many works which for one reason or another could not be discussed in the German edition of this survey nor in the addition which tries to bring this English version up to date. This bibliography added to that in *Treaty and Covenant* will provide a fuller survey of the literature pertaining to the question of the Old Testament covenant than anything else I know of.

PART I: THE TREATIES

I. TEXTS

H. Bengtson, *Die Staatsverträge des Altertums*. II: *Die Verträge der griechisch-römischen Welt von 700 bis 338 v. Chr.*, Munich/Berlin, 1962

R. Borger, 'Zu den Asarhaddon Verträgen aus Nimrud: Nachtrag', *Zeitschrift für Assyriologie* 57 (1964), 261

C. Brekelmans, 'Sefire I A 29–30', *VT* 13 (1963), 223–28

H. Donner and W. Röllig, *Kanaanäische und Aramäische Inschriften*, 3 vols. Wiesbaden, 1962–1964 (Sefire treaties and other relevant records)

J. A. Fitzmyer, S.J., *The Aramaic Inscriptions of Sefire, Biblica et orientalia* 19, Rome, 1967.

H. Freydank, 'Eine hethitische Fassung des Vertrags zwischen dem Hethiter-König Šuppiluliuma und Aziru von Amurru',

Mitteilungen des Instituts für Orientforschung 7 (1960), 357–81.
J. C. Greenfield, 'Three Notes on the Sefire Inscription', *JSS* 11 (1966), 98–105.
H. Klengel, 'Neue Fragmente zur akkadischen Fassung des Aziru-Vertrages', *Orientalische Literatur-Zeitung* 59 (1964), 437–45.
H. Klengel, 'Ein neues Fragment zur historischen Einleitung des Talmišarruma-Vertrages', *Zeitschrift für Assyriologie* 57 (1964), 213–17.
F. W. König, *Die elamischen Königsinschriften, Archiv für Orientforschung Beihefte* 16, Graz, 1965.
J. Nougayrol, *Mission de Ras Shamra IX. Le palais royal d'Ugarit* IV, 2 vols. Paris, 1956.
Erica Reiner, 'The Earliest Elamite Inscription?' *JNES* 24 (1965), 337–40.
E. von Schuler, *Die Kaškäer, Studien zur Assyriologie und vorderasiatischen Archäologie* 3, Berlin, 1965.
I. Sugi, 'Der Vertrag des Tudhalijas IV, mit IŠTAR-muwaš von Amurru', *Orient* (Society for Near Eastern Studies in Japan) 1 (1960), 1–22.
O. Szemerenyi, 'Vertrag des Hethiterkönigs Tudhalija IV mit Ištarmuwa von Amurru', *Oriens antiquus* (*Societas hungarica orientalis*: *Acta*) 9 (1945), 113–29.
K. R. Veenhof, 'An Aramaic Curse with a Sumero-Akkadian Prototype', *Bibliotheca orientalis* 20 (1963), 142–4.
D. J. Wiseman, 'Abban and Alalaḫ', *JCS* 12 (1958), 124–9.

II. STUDIES

G. Buccellati, *Cities and Nations of Ancient Syria, Studi semitici* 26, Rome, 1967.
Cauer, 'Amphiktyonia', Pauly-Wissowa, *Enzyclopädie der Altertumswissenschaft* I.
Karl-Heinz Deller, '*šmn bll* (Hosea 12:2). Additional Evidence', *Biblica* 46 (1965), 349–52.
E. Edel, 'Zur Schwurgötterliste des Hethitervertrags', *Zeitschrift für Ägyptische Sprache und Altertumskunde* 90 (1963), 31–5.
F. C. Fensham, 'The Wild Ass in the Aramaic Treaty between Bar-ga'ayah and Mati'el', *JNES* 22 (1963), 185–6.

J. J. Finkelstein, 'Mesopotamian Historiography', *Proceedings of the American Philosophical Society* 107/6 (1963), 461–72.

G. Furlani, 'I trattati internazionali nell'antichita', *Annuario di diritto comparato e di studi legislativi* 31 (1955), 1–12.

T. Gaster, *Thespis*,² New York, 1961.

I. Gelb, review of D. J. Wiseman, *The Vassal Treaties of Esarhaddon* in *Bibliotheca orientalis* 19 (1962), 159–62.

O. R. Gurney, 'Mita of Paḫḫuwa', *Annals for Archaeology and Anthropology* 28 (1948), 32–47.

H. Güterbok, 'The Deeds of Suppiluliuma as Told by His Son, Mursili II', *JCS* 10 (1946), 41–68, 75–98, 107–30.

M. J. L. Hardy, *Blood Feuds and the Payment of Blood Money in the Middle East*, Beirut, 1963.

W. Hinz, *Das Reich Elam*, Urban Bücher 82, Stuttgart, 1964.

H. Klengel, 'Aziru von Amurru und seine Rolle in der Geschichte der Amarnazeit', *Mitteilungen des Instituts für Orientforschung* 10 (1964), 57–83.

H. Klengel, *Geschichte und Kultur Altsyriens*, Heidelberg, 1967.

H. Klengel, 'Der Scheidsspruch der Muršili II hinsichtlich Barga und seine Übereinkunft mit Duppi-Tešup von Amurru (KBo III.3)', *Orientalia* N. S. 32 (1963), 32–55.

V. Korošec, *Hethitische Staatsverträge*, Leipziger rechtswissenschaftliche Studien 60, Leipzig, 1931.

V. Korošec, 'Keilschriftrecht', *Handbuch der Orientalistik. I. Abteilung, Ergänzungsband* III: *Orientalisches Recht*, Leiden, 1964, 48–215.

M. Liverani, 'Contrasti e confluenze di concezioni politiche nell' età di el-Amarna', *Revue d'assyriologie* 61 (1967), 1–18.

W. L. Moran, 'A Note on the Treaty Terminology of the Sefire Stelas', *JNES* 22 (1963), 173–6.

H. Otten, 'I. Neue Quellen zum Ausgang des hethitischen Reiches', MDOG 94 (1963), 1–23.

H. Otten, 'Ein Kanaanäischer Mythus in Hethischen', *Mitteilungen des Instituts fur Orientforschung* 1 (1953), 125–50.

H. Otten, 'Schrift, Sprache und Literatur der Hethiter', *Historia, Einzelschriften* 7, 11–22.

H. Otten, 'Zwei althethitische Belege zu den Ḫapiru (SA.GAZ)', *Zeitschrift fur Assyriologie* 52 (1957), 216–23.

J. F. Priest, 'ὁρκία in the Iliad and Consideration of a Recent Theory', *JNES* 23 (1964), 48–56.

K. Riemschneider, 'Zum Lehnwesen bei den Hethitern', *Archiv Orientální* 33 (1965), 333–40.

E. von Schuler, 'Staatsverträge und Dokumente hethitischen Rechts', *Historia, Einzelschriften* 7, Wiesbaden, 1964, 34–53.

S. Segert, 'Zur Schrift und Orthographie der altaramäischen Stelen von Sefire', *Archiv Orientální* 32 (1964), 110–26.

E. A. Speiser, 'Cuneiform Law and the History of Civilization', *Proceedings of the American Philosophical Society* 107/6 (1963), 536–41.

H. Tadmor, 'Philistia under Assyrian Rule', *BA* 29 (1966), 86–102.

B. H. Warmington, *Carthage*, London, 1964.

D. B. Weisberg, *Guild Structure and Political Allegiance in Early Achaemenid Mesopotamia*, *Yale Near Eastern Studies* 1, New Haven and London, 1967.

D. B. Weisberg, 'A Neo-Babylonian Temple Report', *JAOS* 87, (1967), 8–12.

G. Walser, ed., *Neuere Hethiterforschung, Historia, Einzelschriften* 7, Wiesbaden, 1964.

PART II: THE OLD TESTAMENT

W. F. Albright, *The Biblical Period from Abraham to Ezra*, New York, 1963.

L. Alonso Schökel, 'Motives sapienciales y de alianza en Gen. 2–3', *Biblica* 43 (1963), 295–316 (= *Theology Digest* 13 (1965), 3–10).

A. Alt, *Essays on Old Testament History and Religion*, Oxford, 1966.

A. Alt, 'The God of the Fathers', *Essays*, 1–100.

A. Alt, 'The Monarchy in the Kingdoms of Israel and Judah', *Essays*, 311–35.

A. Alt, 'The Origins of Israelite Law', *Essays*, 101–72.

A. Alt, 'The Settlement of the Israelites in Palestine', *Essays*, 173–221.

B. W. Anderson, 'The Place of Shechem in the Bible', *BA Reader* 2, 265–75 (= *BA* 20 (1957), 10–19).

Archaeology and Old Testament Study. Jubilee Volume of the Society for Old Testament Study, 1917–1967, ed. D. Winton Thomas, Oxford, 1967.

E. Auerbach, 'Das Zehngebot—Allgemeine Gesetzes-Form in der Bibel', *VT* 16 (1966), 255–76.

K. Baltzer, *Das Bundesformular*, *WMANT* 4, Neukirchen 1964. (ET in preparation, Oxford, 1971.)

J. Begrich, 'Berit. Ein Beitrag zur Erfassung einer alttestamentlichen Denkform', *ZAW* 60 (1944), 1–11 (now in *Gesammelte Studien zum AT*, ed. W. Zimmerli, Munich, 1964, 55–66).

W. Beyerlin, *Origins and History of the Oldest Sinaitic Traditions*. Oxford, 1965. (German, 1961.)

W. Beyerlin, 'Die Paränese im Bundesbuch und ihre Herkunft', *Hertzberg Festschrift*, 9–29.

The Biblical Archaeologist Reader, Vol. 2, edd. E. F. Campbell, Jr. and D. N. Freedman, Garden City, New York, 1964.

J. Blenkinsopp, 'Are there Traces of the Gibeonite Covenant in Deuteronomy?' *CBQ* 28 (1966), 207–19.

J. R. Boston, 'The Wisdom Influence upon the Song of Moses', *JBL* 87 (1968), 198–202.

J. Bright, *A History of Israel*, Philadelphia, 1959.

W. Brueggemann, 'Amos IV 4–13 and Israel's Covenant Worship', *VT* 15 (1965), 1–15.

W. Brueggemann, 'David and His Theologian', *CBQ* 30 (1968), 156–81.

W. Brueggemann, *Tradition for Crisis: A Study in Hosea*, Richmond, Va., 1968.

A. M. Brunet, 'La théologie du Chroniste: théocratie et méssianisme', *Sacra Pagina* 1 (ed. J. Coppens), Gembloux, 1959, 384–97.

P. Buis, 'Les formulaires d'alliance', *VT* 16 (1966), 396–411.

P. Buis and J. Leclercq, *Le Deutéronome, Sources bibliques*, Paris, 1963.

M. J. Buss, 'The Covenant Theme in Historical Perspective', *VT* 16 (1966), 502–4.

P. J. Calderone, S.J., *Dynastic Oracle and Suzerainty Treaty*, *Logos* 1, Manila, 1966.

E. F. Campbell, Jr., 'Shechem in the Amarna Archive', in G. E. Wright, *Shechem*, 191–207.

E. F. Campbell, Jr., and J. F. Ross, 'The Excavation of Shechem and the Biblical Tradition', *BA Reader*, 275–300 (= *BA* 26 (1963), 1–27).

A. Caquot, 'L'alliance avec Abram (Genèse 15)', *Semitica* 12 (1962), 51–66.

A. Caquot, 'La prophétie de Nathan et ses échos lyriques', *VT Suppl.* 9 (1963), 213–24.

H. Cazelles, 'Connexions et structure de Gen. XV', *RB* 69 (1962), 321–49.

H. Cazelles, 'Passages in the Singular within Discourses in the Plural of Deut. 1–4', *CBQ* 29 (1967), 207–19.

H. Cazelles, 'Pentateuque', *Supplément au dictionnaire de la Bible*, VII, Paris, 1964, cols. 736–858.

A. Charbel, *Zebah šᵉlamîm: Il sacrificio pacifico; nei suoi riti e nel suo significato religioso e figurativo*, Jerusalem, 1967.

R. E. Clements, *Abraham and David*, Studies in Biblical Theology 2/5, London, 1967.

R. E. Clements, 'Baal-Berith of Shechem', *JSS* 13 (1968), 21–32.

R. E. Clements, 'Deuteronomy and the Jerusalem Cult Tradition', *VT* 15 (1965), 300–15.

R. E. Clements, *God and Temple. The Idea of the Divine Presence in Ancient Israel*, Oxford, 1965.

R. E Clements, 'The Problem of Old Testament Theology', *The London Quarterly and Holborn Review*, Jan. 1965, 11–17.

R. E. Clements, *Prophecy and Covenant*, Studies in Biblical Theology 43, London, 1965.

J. Coppens, 'La doctrine biblique sur l'amour de Dieu et du prochain', *Ephemerides theologicae lovanienses* 40 (1964), 252–99.

J. Coppens, 'La nouvelle alliance en Jér. 31:31–34', *CBQ* 25 (1963), 12–21.

F. M. Cross, 'Yahweh and the God of the Patriarchs', *Harvard Theological Review* 55 (1962), 225–59.

M. Delcor, 'Les attachés littéraires, l'origine et la signification de l'expression biblique "Prendre à témoin le ciel et la terre" ', *VT* 16 (1966), 8–25.

P. Delhaye, *Le décalogue et sa place dans la morale chrétienne*,[2] Brussels, 1963 (= *L'ami du clergé* 73 (1963), 49–52, 97–101, 199–204, 241–8, 289–91).

R. C. Dentan, 'The Literary Affinities of Exodus XXXIV 6 f.', *VT* 13 (1963), 34–51.

U. Devescovi, O.F.M., *L'alleanza nell'Esateuco*, Macao, 1957.

J. Dus, 'Die altisraelitische amphiktyonische Poesie', *ZAW* 75 (1963), 45–54.

W. Eichrodt, 'Covenant and Law', *Interpretation* 20 (1966), 302–21. (German, *Hertzberg Festschrift*, 30–49).

W. Eichrodt, *Theology of the Old Testament*, 2 vols., London, 1961–1967.

O. Eissfeldt, 'Die älteste Erzählung vom Sinaibund', *ZAW* 73 (1961), 137–46.

O. Eissfeldt, *Die Komposition der Sinai-Erzählung, Exodus 19–34, Sitzungsberichte der Sächsischen Akademie der Wissenschaften, phil.-hist. Kl.*, 113, I, Berlin, 1966.

O. Eissfeldt, 'The Promises of Grace to David in Isaiah 55:1–5', *Muilenburg Festschrift*, 196–207.

D. G. Evans, 'Rehoboam's Advisors at Shechem and Political Institutions in Israel and Sumer', *JNES* 25 (1966), 273–279.

F. C. Fensham, 'Clauses of Protection in Hittite Treaties and in the O.T.', *VT* 13 (1963), 133–43.

F. C. Fensham, 'Covenant, Promise and Expectation in the Bible', *Theologische Zeitschrift* 23 (1967), 305–22.

F. C. Fensham, 'Common Trends in Curses of the Near Eastern Treaties and *Kudurru*—Inscriptions compared with Maledictions of Amos and Isaiah', *ZAW* 75 (1963), 155–75.

F. C. Fensham, 'Did a Treaty between the Israelites and the Kenites Exist?', *BASOR* 175 (1964), 51–4.

F. C. Fensham, 'Maledictions and Benedictions in Ancient Near-Eastern Vassal-Treaties and the Old Testament', *ZAW* 74 (1962), 1–19.

F. C. Fensham, Ps. 21—A Covenant Song', *ZAW* 77 (1965), 193–202.

F. C. Fensham, 'Salt as Curse in the O.T. and the Ancient Near East', *BA* 25 (1962), 49–50.

F. C. Fensham, 'The Treaty between Israel and the Gibeonites', *BA* 27 (1964), 96–100.

F. C. Fensham, 'The Treaty between Solomon and Hiram and the Alalakh Tablets', *JBL* (1960), 59–60.

A. K. Fenz, *Auf Jahwes Stimme hören, Wiener Beiträge zur Theologie* 6, Vienna, 1964.

A. Fitzgerald, 'Hebrew *yd*' = "Love" and "Beloved" ', *CBQ* 29 (1967), 368–74.

G. Fohrer, 'AT—"Amphiktyonie" und "Bund" ', *TLZ* 91 (1966), 802–16, 893–904.

G. Fohrer, 'Das sogenannte apodiktisch formulierte Recht und der Dekalog', *Kerygma und Dogma* 11 (1965), 49–74.

G. Fohrer, 'Remarks on Modern Interpretation of Prophets', *JBL* 80 (1961), 309–19.

G. Fohrer, 'Der Vertrag zwischen König und Volk in Israel', *ZAW* 71 (1959), 1–22.

R. Frankena, 'The Vassal-Treaties of Esarhaddon and the Dating of Deuteronomy', *Oudtestamentische Studien* 14 (1965), 122–54.

D. N. Freedman, 'Divine Commitment and Human Obligation', *Interpretation* 18 (1964), 419–31.

T. E. Fretheim, 'The Ark in Deuteronomy', *CBQ* 30 (1968), 1–14.

T. E. Fretheim, 'Psalm 132: A Form-Critical Study', *JBL* 86 (1967), 289–300.

S. B. Frost, 'The Death of Josiah: A Conspiracy of Silence', *JBL* 87 (1967), 369–82.

N. Fuglister, *Die Heilsbedeutung des Pascha*, SANT 8, Munich, 1963.

B. Gemser, 'The Importance of the Motive Clause in O.T. Law', *VT Suppl.* 1 (1953), 50–66.

B. Gemser, 'The *rîb* or Controversy-Pattern in Hebrew Mentality', *VT Suppl.* (1955), 120–37.

E. Gerstenberger, 'Covenant and Commandment', *JBL* 84 (1965), 38–51.

E. Gerstenberger, *Wesen und Herkunft des 'Apodiktischen Rechts'*, WMANT 20, Neukirchen, 1965.

H. Gese, 'Bemerkungen zur Sinaitradition', *ZAW* 79 (1967), 137–54.

H. Gese, 'Beobachtungen zum Stil alttestamentliche Rechtsatze', *TLZ* 88 (1960), 147–50.

H. Gese, 'Der Davidsbund und die Zionserwählung', *ZTK* 61 (1962), 10–26.

H. Gese, 'The Idea of History in the Ancient Near East and the Old Testament', *Journal for Theology and the Church* 1, New York, 1965, 49–64 (German, *ZTK* 55 (1958), 127–45).

S. Gevirtz, 'Jericho and Shechem: A Religio-Literary Aspect of City Destruction', *VT* 13 (1963), 52–62.

D. Gill, '*Thysia* and *š'lamim*: Questions to R. Schmidt', *Das Bundesopfer in Israel*', *Biblica* 47 (1966), 255–61.

A. González Núñez, 'El Rito de la Alianza', *Estudios Bíblicos* 24 (1966), 217–38.

E. M. Good, 'Hosea 5:8–6:6: An Alternative to Alt', *JBL* 85 (1966), 273–86.

Gottes Offenbarung (Collected Essays of W. Zimmerli), *Theologische Bücherei* 19, Munich, 1963.

J. Gray, 'The Desert Sojourn of the Hebrews and the Sinai-Horeb Tradition', *VT* 4 (1954), 152–3.

J. Gray, 'Ugarit', *Archaeology and Old Testament Study*, 145–67.

J. Gray, *I and II Kings: A Commentary*, London, 1964.

J. Gray, *Joshua, Judges and Ruth. The Century Bible*, new edition London and Edinburgh, 1967.

J. M. Grintz, 'The Treaty of Joshua with the Gibeonites', *JAOS* 86, 113–26.

M. Guilmot, review of L. Delekat, *Katochē*, in *Chronique d'Égypte* 39 (1964), 227–31. (On Gk. *diathēkē* as 'contract' and 'testament'.)

A. H. J. Gunneweg, 'Sinaibund und Davidbund', *VT* 10 (1960), 335–41.

P. B. Harner, 'Exodus, Sinai, and Hittite Prologues', *JBL* 85 (1966), 233–7.

W. Harrelson, 'Shechem in Extra-Biblical References', *BA Reader* 2, 258–65 (= *BA* 20 (1957), 2–10).

J. Harvey, S.J., *Le Plaidoyer prophétique contre Israël après la rupture de l'alliance*, *Studia* 22, Paris and Montreal, 1967.

J. Harvey, S.J., 'Le "*rîb*-Pattern", réquisitoire prophétique sur la rupture de l'alliance', *Biblica* 43 (1962), 172–96.

Jean Héléwa de la Croix, O.C.D., 'Alliance mosaïque et liberté d'Israel', *Ephemerides carmeliticae* 16 (1965), 3–40.

J. Hempel, 'Die israelitischen Anschauungen von Segen und Fluch im Lichte altorientalischer Parallelen', *APOXYSMATA, BZAW* 81 (1961), 30–113.

Edward Heppenstall, 'The Law and the Covenant at Sinai', *St. Andrew's University Studies*[2] (1964), 18–26.

S. Hermann, 'Neuere Arbeiten zur Geschichte Israels', *TLZ* 89 1964), 813–19.

Hertzberg Festschrift: Gottes Wort und Gottes Land, ed. H. Reventlow, Göttingen, 1965.

D. R. Hillers, *Covenant: The History of a Biblical Idea*, Baltimore, 1969.

D. R. Hillers, 'A Note on Some Treaty Terminology in the O.T.', *BASOR* 176 (1964), 46–7.

D. R. Hillers, 'Ritual procession of the Ark in Ps. 132', *CBQ* 30 (1968), 48–55.

D. R. Hillers, *Treaty-Curses and the O.T. Prophets*, Biblica et orientalia 16, Rome, 1964.

H. A. Hoffner, Jr., 'A Hittite Analogue to the David and Goliath Contest of Champions?', *CBQ* 30 (1968), 220–25.

J. Hoftijzer, *Die Verheissungen an die drei Erzväter*, Leiden, 1956.

F. Horst, *Gottes Recht, Theologische Bücherei* 12, Munich, 1961.

F. Horst, 'Der Eid im Alten Testament', *Gottes Recht*, 292–314.

F. Horst, 'Recht und Religion im Bereich des Alten Testaments', *Gottes Recht*, 260–91.

F. Horst, 'Segen und Segenshandlungen in der Bibel', *Gottes Recht*, 188–202.

H. B. Huffmon, 'The Covenant Lawsuit and the Prophets', *JBL* 78 (1959), 286–95.

H. B. Huffmon, 'The Exodus, Sinai and the Credo', *CBQ* 27 (1965), 101–13.

H. B. Huffmon, 'The Treaty Background of Hebrew *Yāda'*', *BASOR* 181 (1966), 31–7.

H. B. Huffmon and S. B. Parker, 'A Further Note on the Treaty Background of Hebrew *Yāda'*', *BASOR* 184 (1966), 36–8.

J. P. Hyatt, 'Moses and the Ethical Decalogue', *Encounter* 26 (1965), 199–206.

W. A. Irwin, 'The Sources of Israel's Faith', *Encounter* 26 (1965), 171–82.

Jörg Jeremias, *Theophanie*, *WMANT* 10, Neukirchen, 1965.

Erich Isaac, 'Circumcision as a Covenant Rite', *Anthropos* 59 (1964), 444–56.

G. Jacob, 'Der Abraham-Bund (Eine Bibelarbeit zu 1. Moses 15)', *Communio viatorum* 7 (1964), 250–4.

A. Jepsen, 'Beiträge zur Auslegung und Geschichte des Dekalogs', *ZAW* 79 (1968), 277–304.

A. Jepsen, 'Berith. Ein Beitrag zur Theologie der Exilzeit', *Rudolph Festschrift*, 161–80.

O. Kaiser, 'Traditionsgeschichtliche Untersuchung von Genesis 15', *ZAW* 70 (1958), 107–26.

A. S. Kapelrud, 'Some Recent Points of View on the Time and Origin of the Decalogue', *Studia Theologica* 18 (1964), 81–90.

Hanna Kassis, 'Gath and the Structure of the "Philistine" Society', *JBL* 84 (1965), 259–71.

R. Kilian, 'Apodiktisches und kasuistisches Recht im Licht ägyptischer Analogien', *BZ* 7 (1963), 185–202.

R. Kilian, *Die vorpriesterlichen Abrahamsüberlieferung*, BBB 24, Bonn, 1966.

E. C. Kingsbury, 'The Theophany *Topos* and the Mountain of God', *JBL* 86 (1967), 205–10.

M. G. Kline, 'Abram's Amen', *Westminster Theological Journal* 31 (1968), 1–11.

M. G. Kline, 'Dynastic Covenant', *Westminster Theological Journal* 23 (1960), 1–15.

M. G. Kline, 'Law Covenant', *Westminster Theological Journal* 27 (1964), 1–20.

M. G. Kline, 'Oath and Ordeal Signs', *Westminster Theological Journal* 27 (1965), 115–39.

M. G. Kline, *Treaty of the Great King*, Grand Rapids, Mich., 1963.

R. Knierim, 'Das erste Gebot', *ZAW* 77 (1965), 20–39.

R. Knierim, *Die Hauptbegriffe für Sünde im Alten Testament*, Gütersloh, 1965.

K. Koch, *The Growth of the Biblical Tradition*, New York, 1969 (Second German edition, Neukirchen, 1967).

L. Köhler, *Old Testament Theology*, London, 1957.

L. Köhler, 'Problems in the Study of the Language of the O.T.', *JSS* 1 (1956), 3–24.

H. J. Kraus, *Worship in Israel*, Oxford, 1966.

E. Kutsch, 'Der Begriff *berît* in vordeuteronomischer Zeit', *Rost Festschrift*, 133–43.

E. Kutsch, 'Gesetz und Gnade. Probleme des alttestamentlichen Bundesbegriff', *ZAW* 79 (1967), 18–35.

E. Kutsch, *Salbung als Rechtsakt im AT und im Alten Orient*, BZAW 87, Berlin, 1963.

I. Lewy, 'The Puzzle of Deut. xxvii: Blessings Announced, but Curses Noted', *VT* 12 (1962), 207–11.

J. L'Hour, 'L'alliance de Sichem', *RB* 69 (1962), 5–36, 161–84, 350–68.

J. L'Hour, *La morale de l'alliance*, Cahiers de la Revue biblique 5, Paris, 1966.

S. Loersch, *Das Deuteronomium und seine Deutungen*, Stuttgarter Bibelstudien 22, Stuttgart, 1967.

N. Lohfink, S.J., 'Der Bundesschluss im Land Moab', *BZ* 6 (1962), 32–56.

N. Lohfink, S.J., 'Die Bundesurkunde des Königs Josias', *Biblica* 44 (1963), 261–88, 461–98.

N. Lohfink, S.J., 'Il "comandamento primo" nell "Antico Testamento" ', *Bibbia e Oriente* 7 (1965), 47–60 (German, 1963).

N. Lohfink, S.J., 'Zur Dekalogfassung von Deut. 5', *BZ* 9 (1965), 17–31.

N. Lohfink, S.J., 'Hate and Love in Osee 9:15', *CBQ* 25 (1963), 417.

N. Lohfink, S.J., *Das Hauptgebot. Eine Untersuchung literarischer Einleitungsfragen zu Dtn 5–11*, Analecta biblica 20, Rome, 1963.

N. Lohfink, S.J., 'Das Hauptgebot', *Siegeslied*, 129–50 (= *Geist und Leben* 36 (1963), 271–81).

N. Lohfink, S.J., 'The Inerrancy and the Unity of Scripture', *Theology Digest* 13 (1965), 185–92.

N. Lohfink, S.J., *Die Landesverheissung als Eid*, Stuttgarter Bibelstudien 28, Stuttgart, 1967.

N. Lohfink, S.J., *Das Siegeslied am Schilfmeer*,[2] Frankfurt a.M., 1966.

N. Lohfink, S.J., 'Die Wandlung des Bundesbegriffs im Buch Dtium', *Rahner Festschrift*, 423–44.

O. Loretz, 'ברית—"Band-Bund" ', *VT* 16 (1966), 239–41.

R. A. F. MacKenzie, S.J., 'The Formal Aspect of Ancient Near Eastern Law', *Meek Festschrift*, 31–44.

D. J. McCarthy, S.J., 'Covenant in the O.T.: The Present State of Inquiry', *CBQ* 27 (1965), 217–40.

D. J. McCarthy, S.J., 'Hosea XII 2: Covenant by Oil', *VT* 14 (1964), 215–21.

D. J. McCarthy, S.J., 'Notes on the Love of God in Deut. and the Father–Son Relationship between Yahweh and Israel', *CBQ* 27 (1965), 144–7.

D. J. McCarthy, S.J., 'II Samuel 7 and the Structure of the Deuteronomic History', *JBL* 84 (1965), 131–8.

D. J. McCarthy, S.J., 'Three Covenants in Genesis', *CBQ* 26 (1964), 179–89.

D. J. McCarthy, S.J., *Treaty and Covenant: A Study in Form in the Ancient Oriental Documents and the O.T.*, Analecta biblica 21, Rome, 1963.

A. Malamat, 'Aspects of the Foreign Policies of David and Solomon', *JNES* 22 (1963), 1–6.

A. Malamat, 'Doctrines of Causality in Hittite and Biblical Historiography', *VT* 5 (1955), 1–12.

A. Malamat, 'Organs of Statecraft in the Israelite Monarchy', *BA* 28 (1965), 34–65.

J. Malfoy, 'Sagesse et loi dans le Deutéronome', *VT* 15 (1965), 49–65.

R. Martin-Achard, 'La nouvelle alliance selon Jérémie', *Revue de theologie et de philosophie*, 3rd series 12 (1962), 81–92.

R. Martin-Achard, 'La signification de l'alliance dans l'Ancien Testament d'après quelques travaux récents', *Revue de theologie et de philosophie*, 3rd series 18 (1968), 88–102.

B. Mazar, 'The Aramaean Empire and its Relations with Israel', *BA* 25 (1962), 98–120.

Meek Festschrift, The Seed of Wisdom, Toronto, 1964.

G. E. Mendenhall, 'Covenant', *The Interpreter's Dictionary of the Bible*, Vol. 1, 714–23.

G. E. Mendenhall, 'The Hebrew Conquest of Palestine', *BA* 25 (1962), 66–87.

G. E. Mendenhall, *Law and Covenant in Israel and the Ancient Near East*, Pittsburgh, Pa., 1955 (= *BA*, 1954).

W. L. Moran, 'The Ancient Near Eastern Background of the Love of God in Dt', *CBQ* 25 (1963), 77–87.

W. L. Moran, 'The Conclusion of the Decalogue (Exod. 20:17, Deut. 5:21)', *CBQ* 29 (1967).

W. L. Moran, 'Moses und der Bundeschluss am Sinai', *Stimmen der Zeit* 170 (1961–62), 120–33 (= *Verbum domini* 40 (1962), 3–17).

W. L. Moran, 'Some Remarks on the Song of Moses', *Biblica* 43 (1962), 317–27.

F. L. Moriarty, S.J., 'Prophets and Covenant', *Gregorianum* 66 (1965), 817–33.

W. Most, 'A Biblical Theology of Redemption in a Covenant Framework', *CBQ* 29 (1967), 1–19.

S. Mowinckel, *Le Décalogue*, Paris, 1927.

S. Mowinckel, *Psalmenstudien*,[2] 5 vols. bound in 2, Amsterdam, 1961. (Originally Oslo, 1921–24).

S. Mowinckel, *The Psalms in Israel's Worship*, 2 vols., New York–Nashville, 1962.

S. Mowinckel, *Zur Frage nach dokumentarischen Quellen in Joshua* 13–19, Oslo, 1946.

Muilenburg Festschrift, Israel's Prophetic Heritage, edd. B. Anderson and W. Harrelson, New York, 1962.

J. Muilenburg, 'The Form and Structure of the Covenantal Formulations', *VT* 9 (1959), 74–9.

J. Muilenburg, 'The "Office" of the Prophet in Ancient Israel', *The Bible in Modern Scholarship* (ed. J. Philip Hyatt), Nashville, 1965, 74–97.

M. L. Newman, *The People of the Covenant: A Study of Israel from Moses to the Monarchy*, London, 1965.

E. W. Nicholson, 'The Centralization of the Cult in Deuteronomy', *VT* 13 (1963), 380–9.

E. W. Nicholson, *Deuteronomy and Tradition*, Oxford, 1967.

E. Nielsen, *The Ten Commandments in New Perspective, Studies in Biblical Theology* 2/7, London, 1968. (German, Copenhagen, 1965.)

E. Norden, *Agnostos Theos*,[4] Stuttgart, 1956. (Important though late material on the theophany.)

R. G. North, S.J., 'The Theology of the Chronicler', *JBL* 82 (1963), 369–81.

M. Noth, *Developing Lines of Theological Thought in Germany*, Annual Bibliographical Lecture 4, Richmond, Va., 1963.

M. Noth, ' "For all who rely on works of the Law are under a curse" ', *Laws in the Pentateuch*, 118–31.

M. Noth, 'God, King, People in the Old Testament: A Methodological Debate with a Contemporary School of Thought', *Journal for Theology and the Church* 1, New York, 1965, 20–48 (German, *ZTK* 47 (1950), 157–91, and see *Laws in the Pentateuch*).

M. Noth, *The History of Israel*[2], Edinburgh, 1960.

M. Noth, *The Laws in the Pentateuch and Other Studies*, Edinburgh, 1966.

M. Noth, 'The Laws in the Pentateuch: Their Assumptions and Meaning', *Laws in the Pentateuch*, 1–107.

M. Noth, 'Old Testament Covenant-Making in the Light of a Text from Mari', *Laws in the Pentateuch*, 108–17.

M. Noth, *Das System der zwölf Stämme Israels, BWANT* IV, 1 Stuttgart, 1930.

F. Nötscher, 'Bundesformular und "Amtsschimmel" ', *BZ* 9 (1965), 182–214.

M. O'Connell, 'The Concept of Commandment in the Old Testament', *Theological Studies* 21 (1961), 351–403.

H. M. Orlinsky, 'The Tribal System of Israel and Related Groups in the Period of the Judges', *Oriens antiquus* 1 (1962), 11–20 (= *Neuman Festschrift*, Leiden, 1962, 375–87).

H. J. Owens, 'Law and Love in Deut.', *Review and Expositor* 61 (1964), 274–83.

A. Penna, 'διαθήκη e συνθήκη nei libri dei Maccabei', *Biblica* 46 (1965), 149–80.

J. Plasteras, *Creation and Covenant*, Contemporary Theology Series, Milwaukee, 1968.

J. Plasteras, *The God of Exodus*, Milwaukee, 1966.

J. Plöger, *Literarkritische, formgeschichtliche und stilkritische Untersuchungen zum Dt., BBB* 26, Bonn, 1967.

N. W. Porteous, 'Actualization and the Prophetic Criticism of the Cult', *Weiser Festschrift*, 93–105.

J. R. Porter, *Moses and Monarchy, A Study in the Biblical Tradition of Moses*, Oxford, 1963.

J. Priest, 'The Covenant of Brothers', *JBL* 84 (1965), 400–6.

C. Rabin, 'Hittite Words in Hebrew', *Orientalia* N.S. 32 (1963), 113–39.

J. J. Rabinowitz, 'Semitic Elements in the Egyptian Adoption Papyrus Published by Gardiner', *JNES* 17 (1958), 145–6. (Gk. *diathēkē* as 'contract' and 'testament'.)

G. von Rad, *Deuteronomy*, London, 1966.

G. von Rad, 'The Form-Critical Problem of the Hexateuch', *Problem of the Hexateuch*, 1–78.

G. von Rad, *Der heilige Krieg im alten Israel, Abhandlungen zur Theologie des Alten und Neuen Testaments* 20, Zurich, 1951.

G. von Rad, *Old Testament Theology*, 2 vols., Edinburgh and London, 1962–1965.

G. von Rad, *The Problem of the Hexateuch and Other Essays*, Edinburgh and London, 1966.

G. von Rad, 'The Royal Ritual in Judah', *Problem of the Hexateuch*, 222-31.

G. von Rad, *Studies in Deuteronomy*, Studies in Biblical Theology 9, London, 1963.

G. von Rad, 'The Tent and the Ark', *Problem of the Hexateuch*, 103-24.

B. D. Rahtjen, 'Philistine and Hebrew Amphictyonies', *JNES* 24 (1965), 100-4.

Rahner Festschrift, Gott im Welt, Freiburg i.B., 1964.

J. Rennes, *Le Deutéronome*, Geneva, 1967.

R. Rentdorff, *Studien zur Geschichte des Opfers im alten Israel*, *WMANT* 24, Neukirchen, 1967.

H. Graf Reventlow, *Gebot und Predigt im Dekalog*, Gutersloh, 1962.

H. Graf Reventlow, 'Kultisches Recht im AT', *ZTK* 60 (1963), 267-304.

H. Graf Reventlow, *Wächter über Israel: Ezechiel und seine Tradition*, *BZAW* 82, Berlin, 1962.

H. Graf Reventlow, *Amos und der prophetische Amt*, Göttingen, 1962.

Ph. Reymond, 'Sacrifice et spiritualité ou sacrifice et alliance? Jer. 7:22-24', *Theologische Zeitschrift* 21 (1965), 314-17.

W. Richter, *Recht und Ethos*, *SANT* 15, 15 Munich, 1966.

M. Roberge, O.M.I., 'Théologie de l'alliance sinaitique dans le Deutéronome', *Revue de l'université d'Ottawa* 34 (1964), 101*-119*, 164*-199*.

H. W. Robinson, *Inspiration and Revelation in the Old Testament*, Oxford, 1946.

Walter R. Roehrs, 'Covenant and Justification in the Old Testament', *Concordia Theological Monthly*, 35 (Oct. 1964), 583-602 (= 'Das alttestamentliche Bund und die Rechtfertigung durch den Glauben', *Lutherischer Rundblick* 12 (1964), 154-72).

Rost Festschrift, Das ferne und nahe Wort, *BZAW* 105, ed. F. Maass, Berlin, 1967.

L. Rost, 'Erwägungen zu Hos. 4:13 f.', *Bertholet Festschrift* (edd. W. Baumgartner, O. Eissfeldt, etc.), Tubingen, 1950, 451-60.

L. Rost, *Das kleine Credo und andere Studien zum Alten Testament*, Heidelberg, 1965.

L. Rost, 'Das kleine geschichtliche Credo', *Das kleine Credo*, 11-24.

L. Rost, 'Sinaibund und Davidsbund', *TLZ* (1947), 129–34.

H. H. Rowley, *Men of God, Studies in OT History and Prophecy*, London, 1963.

J. Scharbert, *Heilsmittler im Alten Testament und im Alten Orient, Quaestiones disputate* 23–4, Freiburg i.B., 1964.

Cl. Schedl, 'Die heilsgeschichtliche Funktion der Propheten', *Bibel und Kirche* 19 (1964), 9–12.

R. Schmid, *Das Bundesopfer in Israel, SANT* 9, Munich, 1964.

G. Schmitt, 'El Berit—Mitra', *ZAW* 76 (1964), 325–7.

G. Schmitt, *Der Landtag zu Sichem, Arbeiten zur Theologie* 1/15, Stuttgart, 1964.

W. Schottroff, *'Gedenken' im Alten Orient und im AT, WMANT* 15, Neukirchen, 1964.

K. D. Schunk, 'Die Richter Israels und ihr Amt', *VT Suppl.* 15, Leiden, 1966, 252–62.

Masao Sekine, 'Davidsbund und Sinaibund bei Jeremia', *VT* 9 (1959), 47–57.

L. Sirard, 'Sacrifices et rites sanglants dans l'Ancien Testament', *Sciences ecclésiastiques* 15 (1963), 163–98.

R. Smend, *Die Bundesformel, Theologische Studien* 68, Zurich, 1963.

R. Smend, *Jahwekrieg und Stämmebund, FRLANT* 84, Göttingen, 1966.

R. H. Smith, 'Abram and Melchizedek', *ZAW* 77 (1965), 129–53.

J. A. Soggin, 'Zwei umstrittene Stellen aus dem Überlieferungskreis um Shechem', *ZAW* 74 (1961), 78–87.

J. J. Stamm and M. E. Andrew, *The Ten Commandments in Recent Research, Studies in Biblical Theology* 2/2, London, 1967.

S. Šveda, 'Der Bund, das Gesetz und die Propheten', *Bibel und Kirche* 19 (1964), 5–9.

J. Swetnam, S.J., *'Diathēkē* in the Septuagint Account of Sinai: A Suggestion', *Biblica* 47 (1966), 438–44.

J. A. Thompson, *The Ancient Near Eastern Treaties and the Old Testament*, London, 1964.

J. A. Thompson, 'The Near Eastern Suzerain-Vassal Concept in the Religion of Israel', *The Journal of Religious History* 3 (1964), 1–19.

J. A. Thompson, 'Non-Biblical Covenants in the Ancient Near

East and their Relevance for Understanding the Covenant Motif in the O.T.', *Australian Biblical Review* 8 (1960), 39–45.

J. A. Thompson, 'The Significance of the Ancient Near Eastern Treaty Pattern', *The Tyndale House Bulletin* (Cambridge, Eng.) 13 (1963), 1–6.

T. C. G. Thornton, 'Charismatic Kingship in Israel and Judah', *JTS* n.s. 14 (1963), 1–11.

L. E. Toombs, 'Love and Justice in Deuteronomy', *Interpretation* 19 (1965), 389–411.

M. Tsevat, 'The Neo-Assyrian and Neo-Babylonian Vassal Oaths and the Prophet Ezekiel', *JBL* 78 (1959), 199–204.

Gene M. Tucker, 'Covenant Forms and Contract Forms', *VT* 15 (1965), 487–503.

Gene M. Tucker, 'The Legal Background of Genesis 23', *JBL* 85 (1966), 77–84.

Gene M. Tucker, 'Witnesses and "Dates" in Israelite Contracts', *CBQ* 28 (1966), 42–5.

R. de Vaux, O.P., 'Bulletin', *RB* 74 (1967), 286.

R. de Vaux, O.P., 'The Hebrew Patriarchs and History', *Theology Digest* 12 (1964), 227–40.

R. de Vaux, O.P., 'Le roi d'Israël, vassal de Yahwé', *Tisserant Festschrift, Studi e testi* 231, Vatican City, 1964, 119–33.

K. R. Veenhof, review of E. Kutsch, *Salbung als Rechtsakt im Alten Testament und im alten Orient* in *Bibliotheca orientalis* 23 (1966), 308–13.

E. von Waldow, *Der Traditionsgeschichtliche Hintergrund der prophetischen Gerichtsreden*, *BZAW* 85, Berlin, 1963.

M. Weinfeld, 'Deuteronomy—The Present State of Inquiry', *JBL* 86 (1967), 249–62.

M. Weinfeld, 'Traces of Assyrian Formulae in Deuteronomy', *Biblica* 46 (1965), 417–27.

M. Weippert, *Die Landnahme der israelitischen Stämme in der neueren wissenschaftlichen Diskussion*, *FRLANT* 92, Göttingen, 1967.

Weiser Festschrift, Tradition und Situation, edd. E. Wurthwein and O. Kaiser, Berlin, 1963.

A. Weiser, *The Old Testament: Its Formulation and Development*, London, 1961.

A. Weiser, *The Psalms*, London, 1962.

A. Weiser, *Samuel. Seine geschichtliche Aufgabe und religiose Bedeutung*, FRLANT 81, Göttingen, 1962.

C. F. Whitley, 'Covenant and Commandment in Israel', *JNES* 22 (1963), 37-48.

G. Widengren, 'King and Covenant', *JSS* 2 (1957), 1-32.

H. Wildberger, *Jahwes Eigentumsvolk*, *ATANT* 37, Zürich-Stuttgart, 1960.

F. Willesen, 'Die Eselsohne von Sichem als Bundesgenossen', *VT* 4 (1954), 216-17.

J. Wijngaards, 'Death and Resurrection in Covenantal Context (Hos. VI 2)', *VT* 17 (1967), 226-7.

J. Wijngaards, *The Formulas of the Deuteronomic Creed*, Tilburg, Netherlands, 1963.

J. G. Williams, 'Concerning one of the Apodictic Formulas', *VT* 14 (1964), 484-9.

D. J. Wiseman, 'Alalakh', *Archaeology and Old Testament Study*, 119-35.

G. E. Wright, 'The Lawsuit of God: A Form-Critical Study of Deut. 32', *Muilenburg Festschrift*, New York, 1962, 26-67.

G. E. Wright, 'Shechem', *Archaeology and Old Testament Study*, 355-69.

G. E. Wright, *Shechem, The Biography of a Biblical City*, New York and Toronto, 1965.

W. Zimmerli, 'Das Gesetz im AT', *Gottes Offenbarung*, 249-76.

W. Zimmerli, 'Ich bin Jahwe', *Gottes Offenbarung*, 11-40.

W. Zimmerli, *The Law and the Prophets*, Oxford, 1965.

W. Zimmerli, 'Promise and Fulfilment', *Essays in O.T. Hermeneutics* (edd. C. Westermann and J. L. Mays), Richmond, Va., 1963, 89-122 (= *Evangelische Theologie* 12 (1952-53), 34-59).

W. Zimmerli, 'Sinaibund und Abrahambund', *Gottes Offenbarung*, 205-16.

Index of Authors

Index of Subjects